SOUTH EAST ENGL...
Regional Road Atlas

CW00386496

CONTENTS

REFERENCE

MOTORWAY	**M1**
Under Construction	
Proposed	
MOTORWAY JUNCTIONS WITH NUMBERS	
Unlimited interchange **4** Limited interchange **8**	
MOTORWAY SERVICE AREA	**FERRYBRIDGE**
with acces from one carriageway only	Ⓢ
	Ⓢ
MAJOR ROAD SERVICE AREAS	**LEEMING** **GRASBY**
with 24 hour Facilities	Ⓢ Ⓢ
PRIMARY ROUTE	**A19**
PRIMARY ROUTE DESTINATION	**DOVER**
DUAL CARRIAGEWAY (A & B Roads)	
CLASS A ROAD	A614
CLASS B ROAD	B6422
MAJOR ROAD UNDER CONSTRUCTION	
MAJOR ROAD PROPOSED	
GRADIENT 1:5 (20%) & STEEPER	«
(Ascent in direction of arrow)	
TOLL	*TOLL*
MILEAGE BETWEEN MARKERS	8
RAILWAY AND STATION	
LEVEL CROSSING AND TUNNEL	
RIVER OR CANAL	
COUNTY OR UNITARY AUTHORITY BOUNDARY	
NATIONAL BOUNDARY	—+—+
BUILT UP AREA	
VILLAGE OR HAMLET	○
WOODED AREA	
SPOT HEIGHT IN FEET	• 813
HEIGHT ABOVE 400' - 1,000' ___ 122m - 305m ___	
SEA LEVEL 1,000' - 1,400' ___ 305m - 427m ___	
1,400' - 2,000' ___ 427m - 610m ___	
2,000'+ ___ 610m + ___	
NATIONAL GRID REFERENCE (Kilometres)	100

TOURIST INFORMATION

AIRPORT	✈
AIRFIELD	✈
HELIPORT	🚁
BATTLE SITE AND DATE	⚔ *1408*
CASTLE (Open to Public)	🏰
CASTLE WITH GARDEN (Open to Public)	🏰
CATHEDRAL, ABBEY, FRIARY, PRIORY, CHURCH (Open to Public)	✝
COUNTRY PARK	⍾
FERRY (Vehicular) ___ 🚢 🚢 (Foot only) ___	⛴
GARDEN (Open to Public)	✼
GOLF COURSE ___ 9 HOLE ___ 18 HOLE ___	⛳
HISTORIC BUILDING (Open to Public)	🏛
HISTORIC BUILDING WITH GARDEN (Open to Public)	🏛
HORSE RACECOURSE	🏇
INFORMATION CENTRE, VISITOR CENTRE OR TOURIST INFORMATION CENTRE	🛈
LIGHTHOUSE	🗼
MOTOR RACING CIRCUIT	
MUSEUM, ART GALLERY	🖼
NATIONAL PARK OR FOREST PARK	
NATIONAL TRUST PROPERTY (Open)	*NT*
(Restricted Opening)	*NT*
NATURE RESERVE OR BIRD SANCTUARY	
NATURE TRAIL OR FOREST WALK	
PLACE OF INTEREST ___ *Monument*	•
PICNIC SITE	⊼
RAILWAY (Preserved, Miniature, Steam or Narrow Gauge)	🚂
TELEPHONE ___ PUBLIC (Selection) ___ ✆ AA OR RAC ___	✆
THEME PARK	
VIEWPOINT	⁂
WILDLIFE PARK	
WINDMILL	
ZOO OR SAFARI PARK	🐘

SCALE

```
0    1    2    3    4    5    6 Miles
0  1  2  3  4  5  6  7  8  9  10 Kilometres
```

1:158,400
2.5 Miles to 1 Inch

Geographers' A-Z Map Company Ltd

Head Office : Fairfield Road,
Borough Green, Sevenoaks, Kent TN15 8PP
Telephone: 01732- 781000

Showrooms :
44 Gray's Inn Road, London, WC1X 8HX
Telephone: 020- 7440 9500

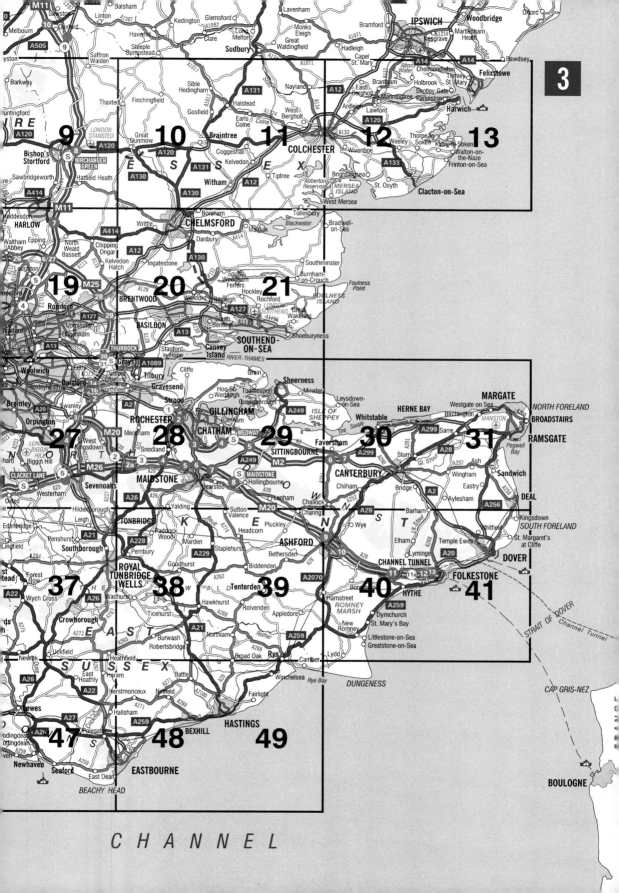

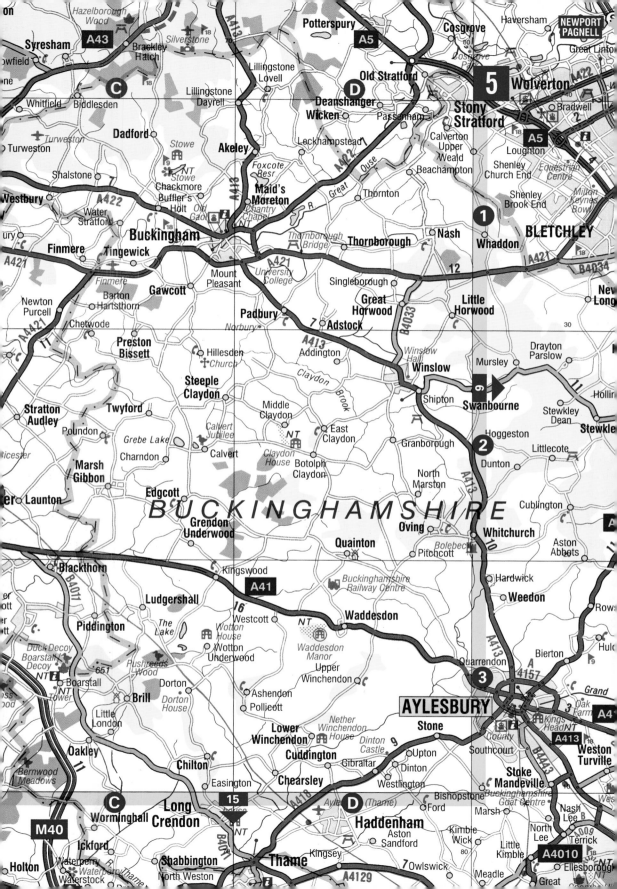

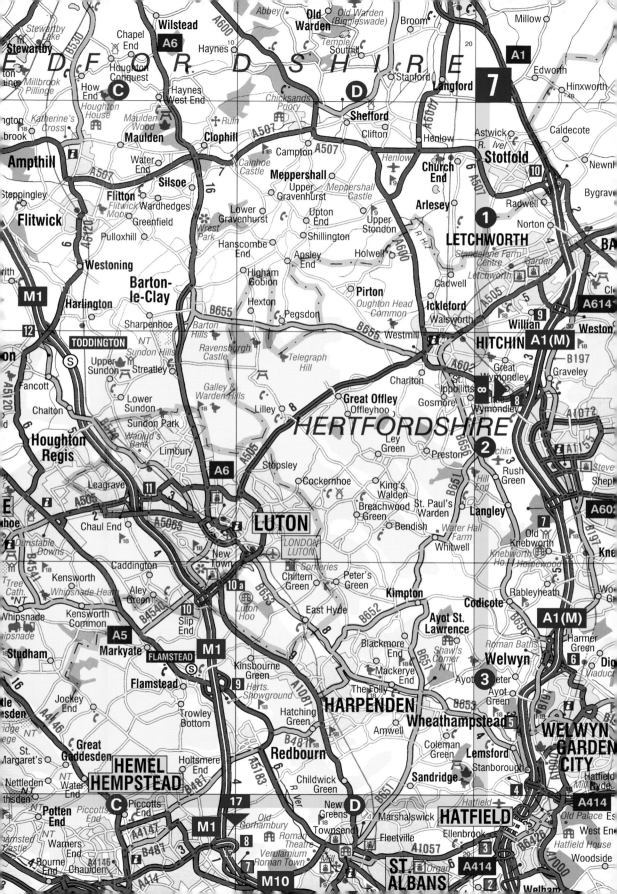

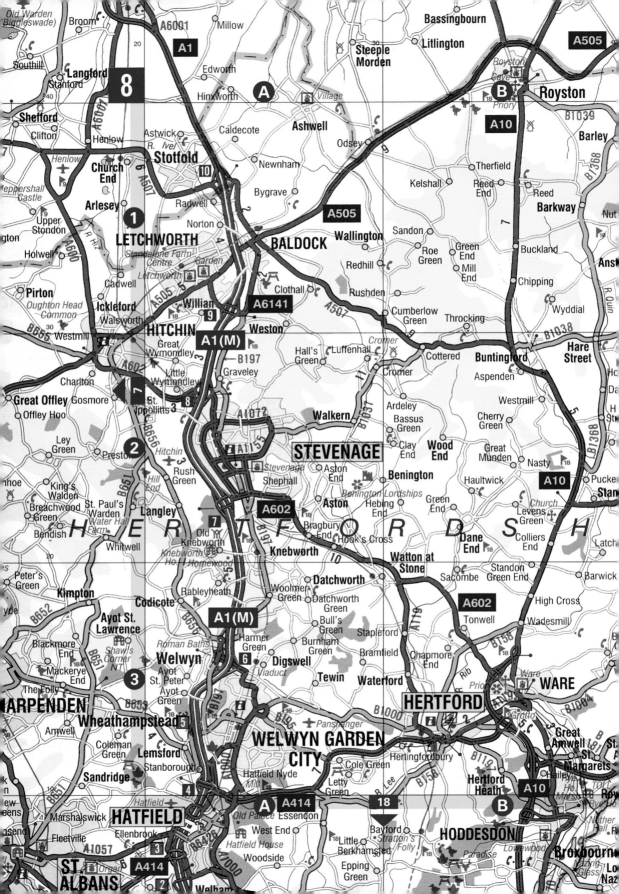

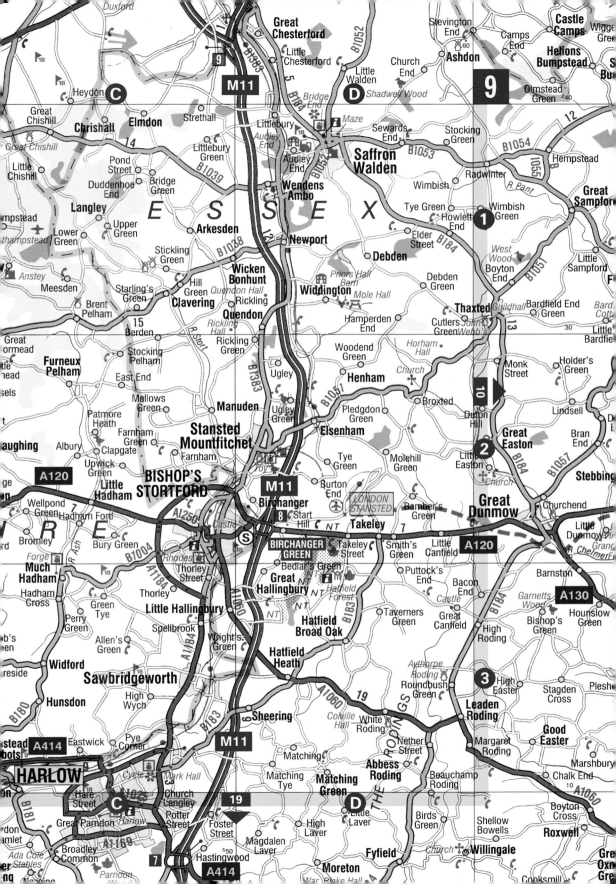

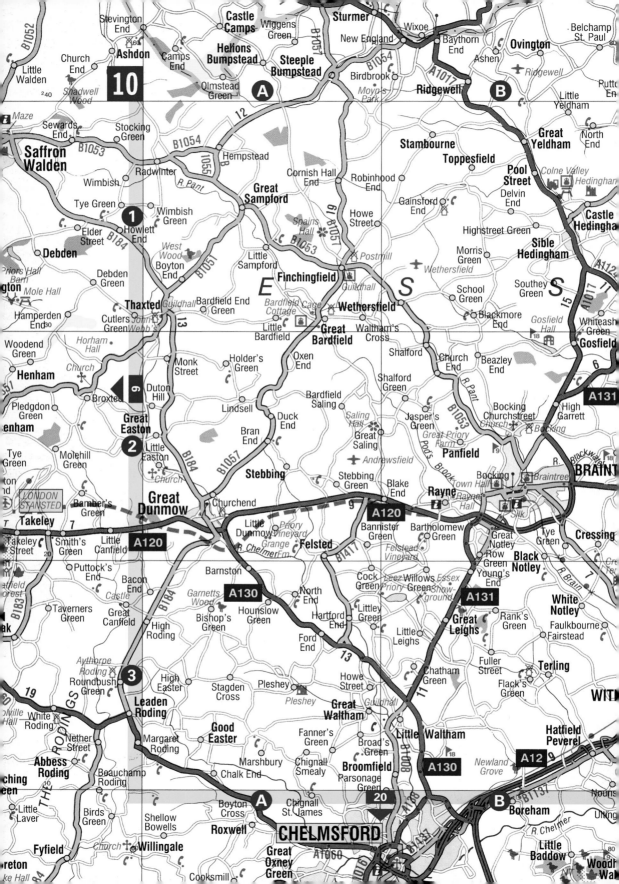

Little Walden
Stevington End
Ashdon
Camps End
Church End
Castle Camps
Wiggens Green
Helions Bumpstead
Steeple Bumpstead
Olmstead Green
Sturmer
New England
Wixoe
Baythorn End
Ashen
Ovington
Belchamp St. Paul
Birdbrook
Moyn's Park
Ridgewell
Ridgewell
Great Yeldham
North End
Little Yeldham
Putto En

A
B

240
Shadwell Wood

Maze
Sewards End
Stocking Green
B1054
Hempstead
Cornish Hall End
Stambourne
Toppesfield
Pool Street
Colne Valley
Hedingha
Saffron Walden
B1053
Radwinter
R. Pant
1055
Great Sampford
Robinhood End
Gainsford End
Delvin End
Castle Hedingha
Wimbish
Tye Green
Howlett End
Wimbish Green
Spains Hall
Howe Street
B1053
Highstreet Green
Morris Green
Sible Hedingham
Southey Green
A112
Elder Street
B184
West Wood
Boyton End
Little Sampford
Finchingfield
Postmill
Wetherfield
School Green
A1017
Debden
Debden Green
Guildhall
E
S
S
Blackmore End
Gosfield Hall
Whiteash Green
Gosfield
Priors Hall Barn
Mole Hall
Thaxted
Bardfield End Green
Bardfield Cage
Bardfield Cottage
Great Bardfield
Waltham's Cross
Shalford
Church End
Beazley End
High Garrett
A131
Hamperden End
Cutlers Green
John Webb's
Little Bardfield
Oxen End
Shalford Green
Bocking Churchstreet
Bocking
6
Woodend Green
Horham Hall
Church
Monk Street
Holder's Green
Bardfield Saling
Jasper's Green
B1053
Great Priory Farm
Henham
Broxted
Duton Hill
Lindsell
Duck End
Saling Hall
Great Saling
Andrewsfield
Panfield
Pledgdon Green
enham
Great Easton
Little Easton
Bran End
Stebbing
Stebbing Green
Blake End
Rayne
Bocking
Town Hall
Braintree
BRAINT
Tye Green
Molehill Green
Church
B184
B1057
Churchend
Great Dunmow
Little Dunmow
Bannister Green
Bartholomew Green
Rayne Hall
Silk
Cressing
Takeley
Smith's Green
Bamber's Green
Little Canfield
A120
Priory Vineyard
Grange
Felsted
Cock Green
Felstead Vineyard
Great Notley
Young's End
Tye Green
Black Notley
R. Brain
Puttock's End
Castle
Bacon End
Barnston
B1417
Leez Willows
Priory Green
Essex Showground
A131
White Notley
Tavemers Green
Great Canfield
High Roding
Garnetts Wood
Bishop's Green
Hounslow Green
North End
Hartford End
Littley Green
Great Leighs
Rank's Green
Faulkbourne
Fairstead
B184
A130
Ford End
Little Leighs
Fuller Street
Terling
Aythorpe Roding
Roundbush Green
High Easter
Stagden Cross
Pleshey
Howe Street
Chatham Green
Flack's Green
WITH
Leaden Roding
Pleshey
Great Waltham
Guildhall
Hatfield Peverel
A12
Nether Street
Margaret Roding
Good Easter
Fanner's Green
Broad's Green
Little Waltham
Newland Grove
A130
Abbess Roding
Beauchamp Roding
Marshbury
Chignall Smealy
Broomfield
Parsonage Green
B1008
ching en
White Roding
Birds Green
Shellow Bowells
Boyton Cross
Chignall St. James
Great Oxney Green
CHELMSFORD
Boreham
R. Chelmer
Little Baddow
Woodr Wa
Little Laver
Fyfield
Roxwell
Willingale
Cooksmill
A1060

THE RODINGS

1
2
3
6

LONDON STANSTED

A120
A130
A131
A12

9
13
11
20

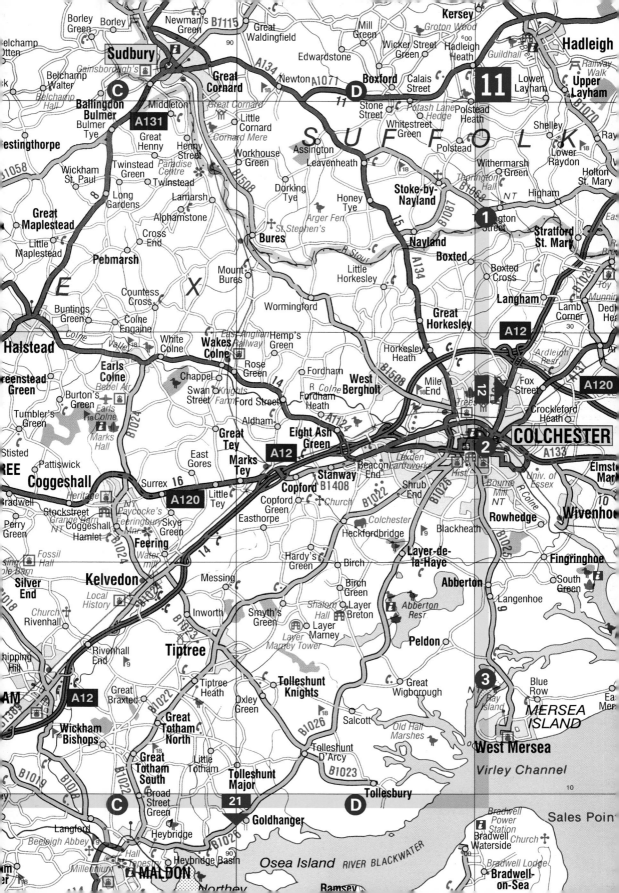

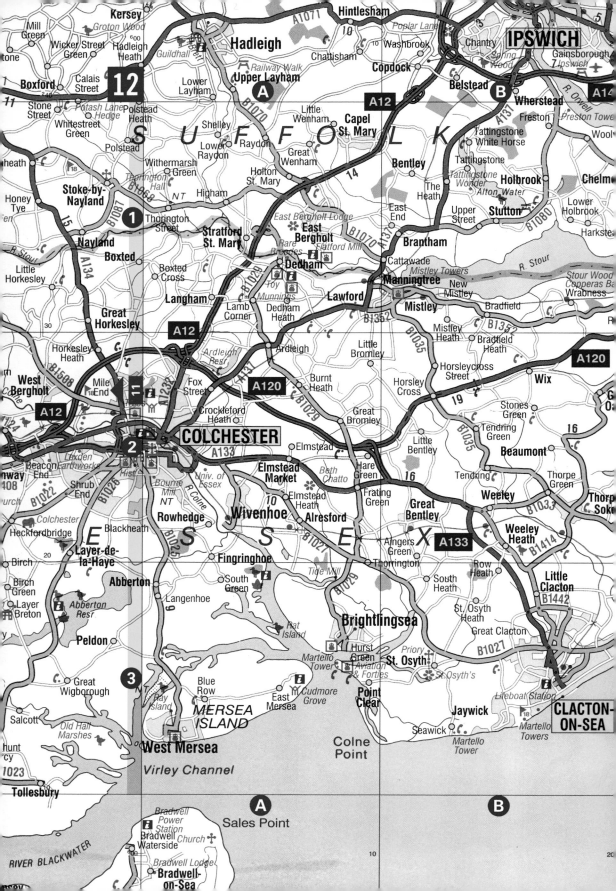

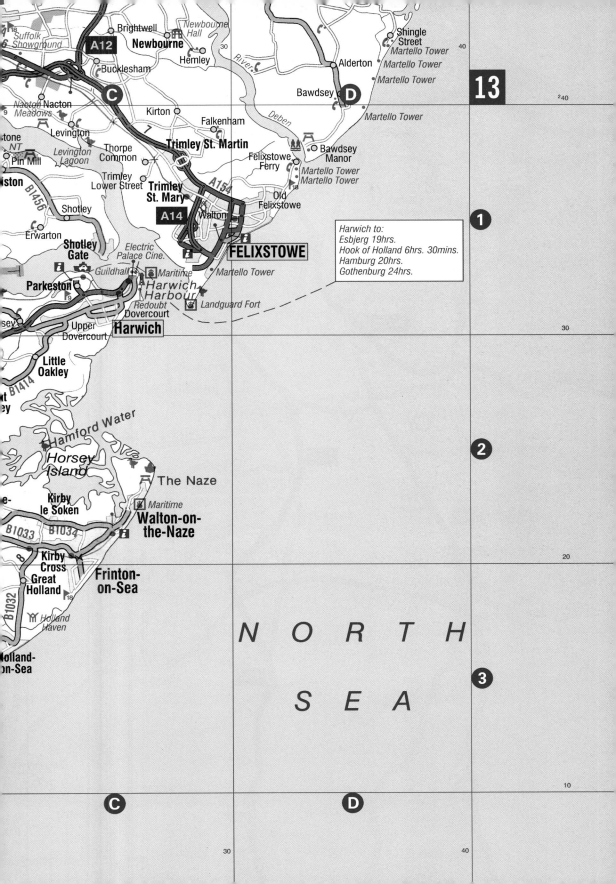

13

Brightwell
Newbourne Hall
Newbourne
Hemley
A12
Suffolk Showground
Bucklesham
Shingle Street
Martello Tower
Alderton
Martello Tower
Bawdsey
Martello Tower
C
Nacton Nacton
Meadows
Kirton
Falkenham
D
River *Deben*
Levington
Thorpe Common
Trimley St. Martin
Martello Tower
Felixstowe Ferry
Levington Lagoon
NT
Pin Mill
Trimley Lower Street
Trimley St. Mary
Old Felixstowe
Martello Tower
Martello Tower
Bawdsey Manor
Shotley
A154
Walton
Erwarton
A14
B1456
Shotley Gate
Electric Palace Cine.
FELIXSTOWE
Martello Tower
Guildhall
Maritime
Parkeston
Harwich Harbour
Landguard Fort
Redoubt
Upper Dovercourt
Dovercourt
Harwich

> Harwich to:
> *Esbjerg 19hrs.*
> *Hook of Holland 6hrs. 30mins.*
> *Hamburg 20hrs.*
> *Gothenburg 24hrs.*

1

Little Oakley
B1414

Hamford Water

2

Horsey Island
The Naze
Kirby le Soken
Maritime
B1033 B1034
Walton-on-the-Naze
Kirby Cross
Great Holland
Frinton-on-Sea
B1032

3

Holland Haven

Holland-on-Sea

N O R T H

S E A

C

D

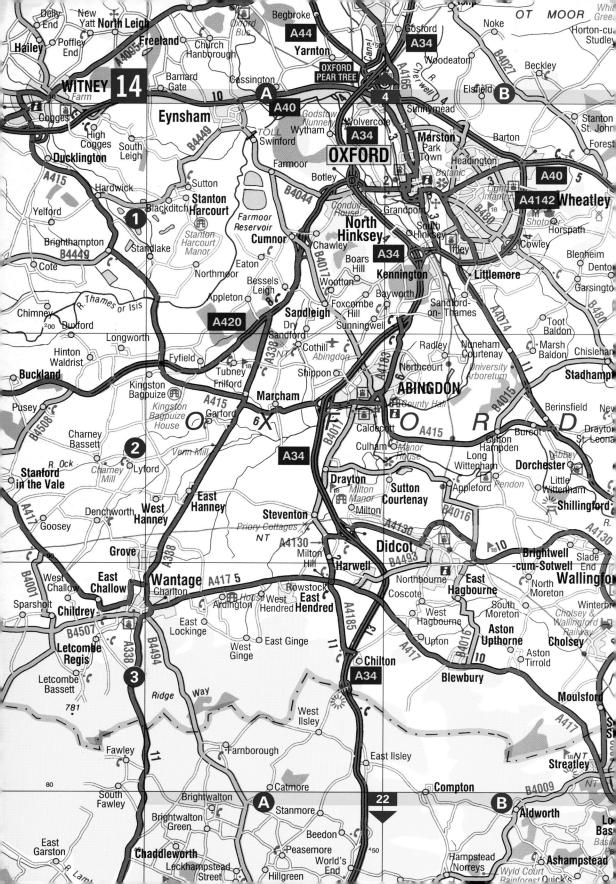

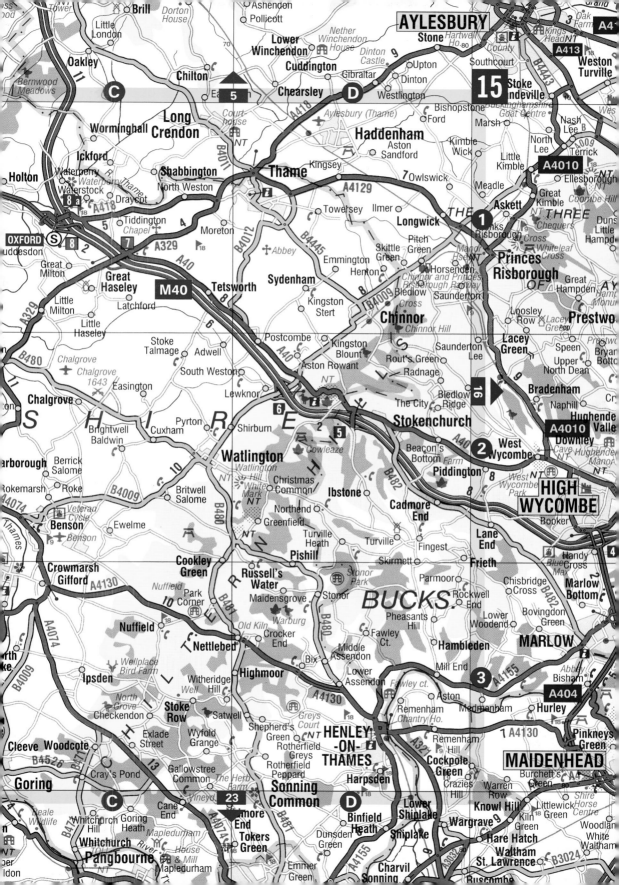

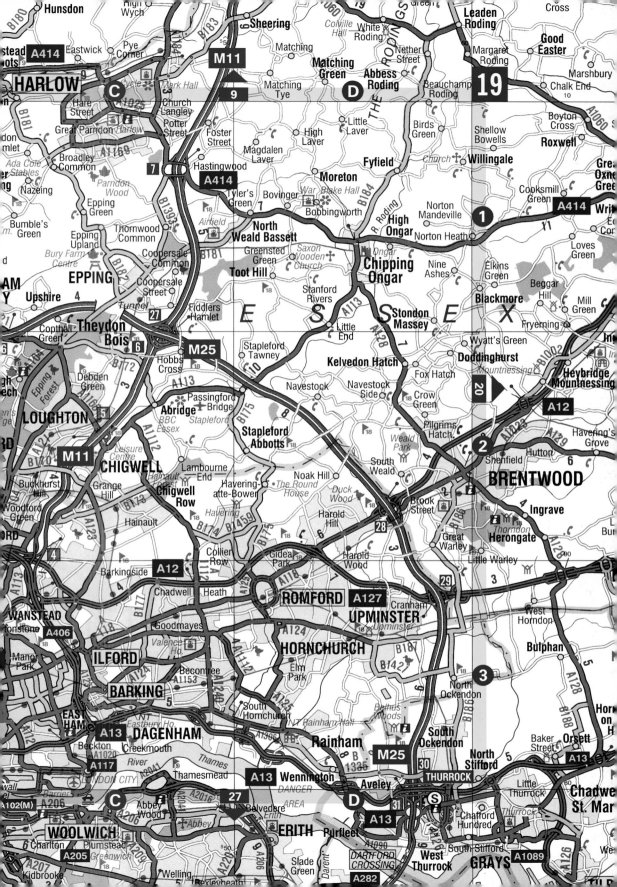

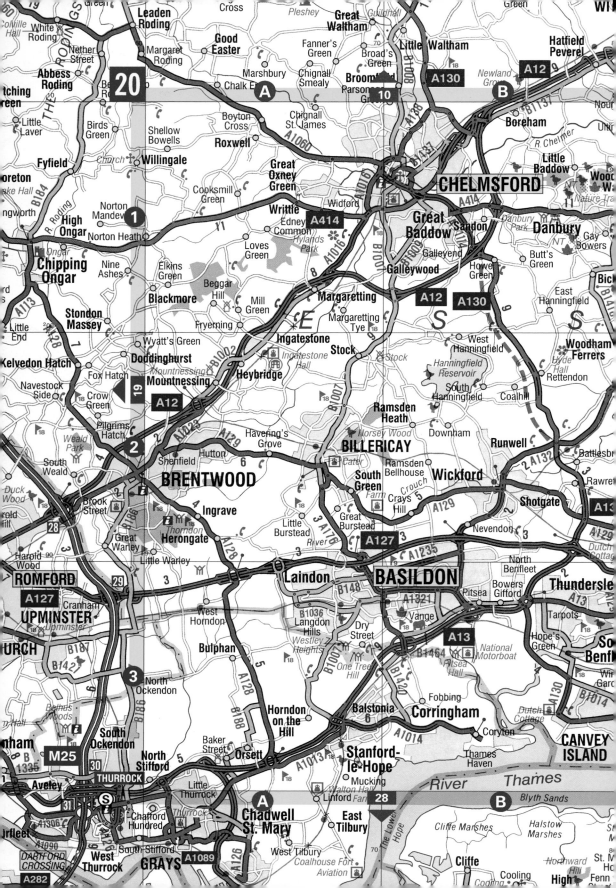

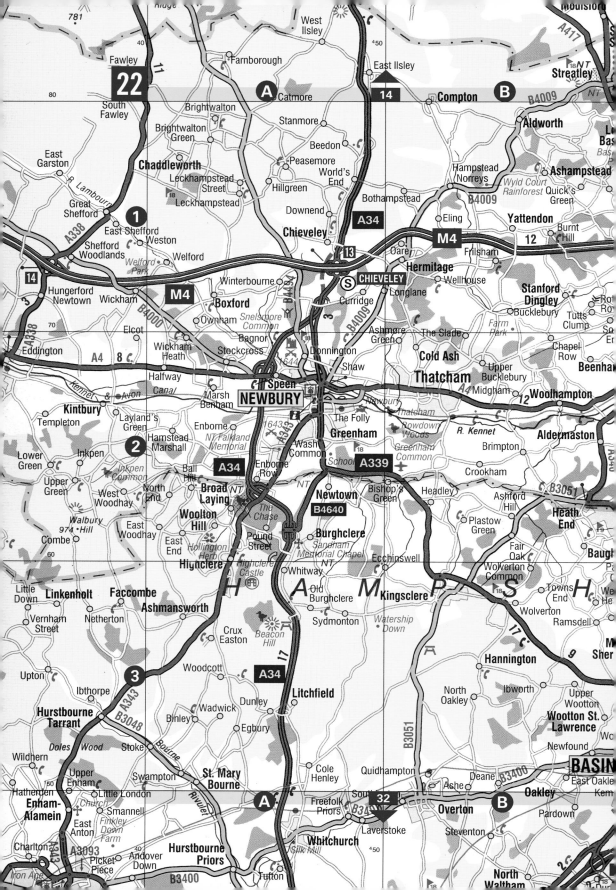

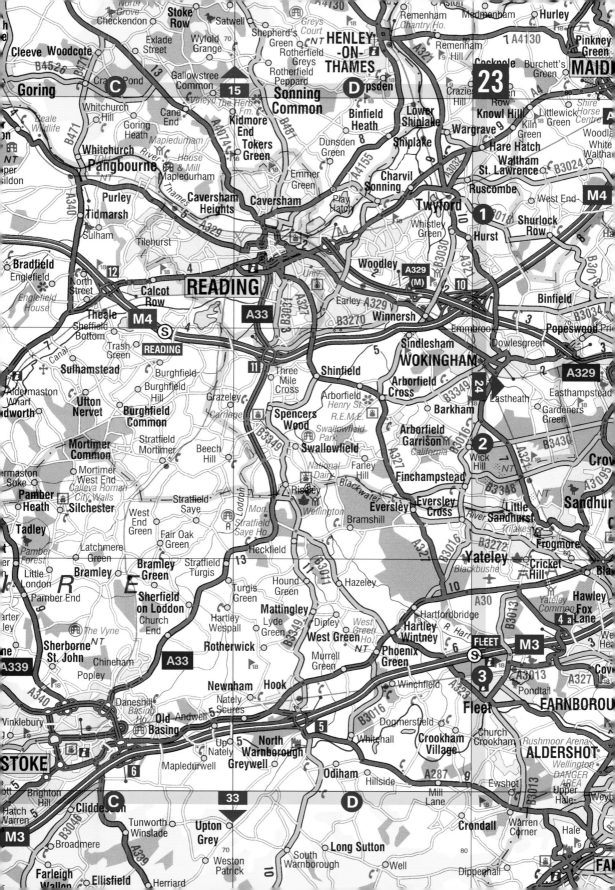

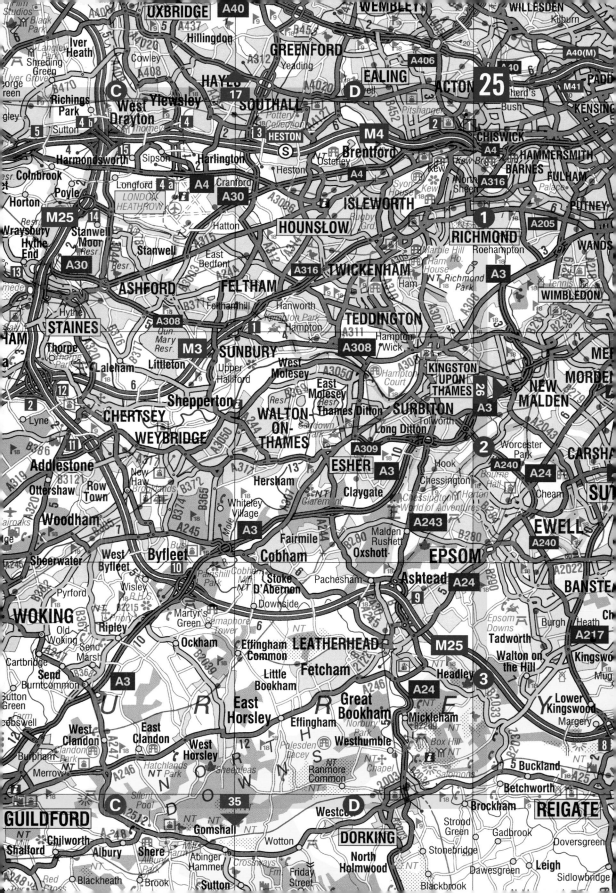

A   B

SHEERNESS

Minster

East End

Coastal Park

Gatehouse

B2008

Eastchurch

Warden

Warden Point

Brambledown

B2231

Leysdown-on-Sea

ISLE   **OF**   **SHEPPEY**

Leysdown Coastal Park

Herne Bay

mley and

Elmley Marshes

Isle of Harty

Shell Ness

The Swale

HERNE BAY

Hampton

The Swale

WHITSTABLE

Tankerton

Swalecliffe

The

Swale

Whitstable Bay

Chestfield

5

Greenhill

Herne

& Kemsley Railway

South Swale Nature Reserve

Seasalter

South Street

West End

Herne Common

Mayp

on Sailing Barge

Conyer

Uplees

South Swale

Oare Marshes

Graveney

Yorkletts

5

Brambles Wildlife Park

A291

OURNE

Teynham Street

Oare

Denstroude

Clowes Wood

Bird Garden

Calcott

Sturry

He

Castle

Teynham

Luddenham

Heritage Centre

A299

Dargate

Honey Hill

Broad Oak

sham

Lynsted

Lewson Street

Goodnestone

Homestall Farm

Hernhill

Blean Wood

Blean

Tyler Hill

University of Kent

CANTERBU

West

FAVERSHAM

Preston

Osprenge

Mount Ephraim

Boughton under Blean

Church Wood

Fordwi

A290

Fordwi

M2

Newnham

Painter's Forstal

North Street

A251

2

7

A2

Dunkirk

7

Rough Common

Harbledown

A28

Littlebo

A257

Doddington Place

Prospect Tower

Hogben's Hill

South Street

Oversland

Thanington

A2050

Howletts Zoo Park

Patrix

dington

Eastling

Belmont

Sheldwich

Sheldwich Lees

Selling

Chartham Hatch

A2

Nackington

Bridge

Throwley

Perrywood

Perry Wood

Old Wives Lees

Chartham

Lower Hardres

Bridge

3

Badlesmere

Shottenden

Bagham

Shalmsford Street

Bishopsbourne

Throwley Forstal

Leaveland

Park Wood

Chilham

Watermill

Garlinge Green

Petham

Kingston

Stalisfield Green

A252

Chilham Castle

Denge Wood

Earley Wood

B2068

Bar

D

12

14

Molash

King's Wood

Godmersham

Wye (Crundale Downs)

Stocker's Head

Challock

A252

A251

A

Bill

40

Waltham

Bossingham

Derringsto

Paddock

The Lees

Boughton Aluph

Crundale

Street

Yockletts Bank

ring

ing

ath

Archbishop's Palace

Challock

A28

Stour

Wye Crown Memorial

Hassell Street

North Leigh

Stelling Minnis

Elham Val Vineyard

Westwell Leacon

Westwell

Boughton Lees

Goat Lees

Wye

Bodsham

Stelling Minnis

Park Gate Down

Little Chart

Ram Lane

Ram

1

South Channel

Lifeboat House

MARGATE   Foreness Point

Westgate on Sea   Westbrook   Cliftonville   Kingsgate

Minnis Bay   Tudor B20

Reculver Towers   Reculver   Dreamland   NORTH FORELAND

Regulbium Roman Fort   Birchington   St. Peter's   Bleak House   BROADSTAIRS

Hillborough   A299   A28   Quex House   Westwood   Dickens House

roomfield   B2048   ISLE OF   Northwood

St. Nicholas   Acol   THANET   4

at Wade   B2050   Manston   A256

Boyden Gate   Monkton   5   Manston   A253

Sarre   A253   Monkton   Cliffs   2   RAMSGATE

Chislet   End   Rural   A256   Motor

Upstreet   West   Minster   Life

Stourmouth   Ebbsfleet   NT

Stodmarsh   East   R. Stour   Pegwell   **2**

Stodmarsh   Stourmouth   Bay

Grove   Richborough   NT

Preston   Westmarsh   Paramour   Castle   Richborough

Ware   Street   Port

Elmstone   Goldstone   60

Wickhambreaux   Hoaden   Amphitheatre   Great Stonar

Nash   Cooper   White

Ickham   Street   Sandwich   Sandwich

Wingham   Ash   A257   Guildhall   Bay

Bramling   Bird Park   Marshborough   TOLL

sbourne   Staple   Vineyard   Woodnesborough   Worth

Adisham   Goodnestone   Hammill   The Small   **3**

Park   Eastry   Ham   Downs

Goodnestone   Heronden   A258   Sandown

Chillenden   Finglesham   Local

Nonington   Knowlton   Betteshanger   History   Victoriana

Aylesham   Easole   Northbourne   Time-Ball   The

Street   Sholden   Tower   Downs

B2046   Frogham   Tilmanstone   Northbourne Ct.   DEAL

Womenswold   Elvington   11   Deal

Great

Barfrestone   A256   Mongeham   Walmer

East Kent Light   Ripple   150

Woolage   Eythorne   41   Sutton   Walmer

Green   Ashley   Ringwould   Kingsdown

Shepherdswell   West   NT

or Sibertswold   Langdon   DANGER   60

Coldred   Martin   AREA

A260   Martin Mill   The

Wootton   East   Dover Patrol Monument

Langdon

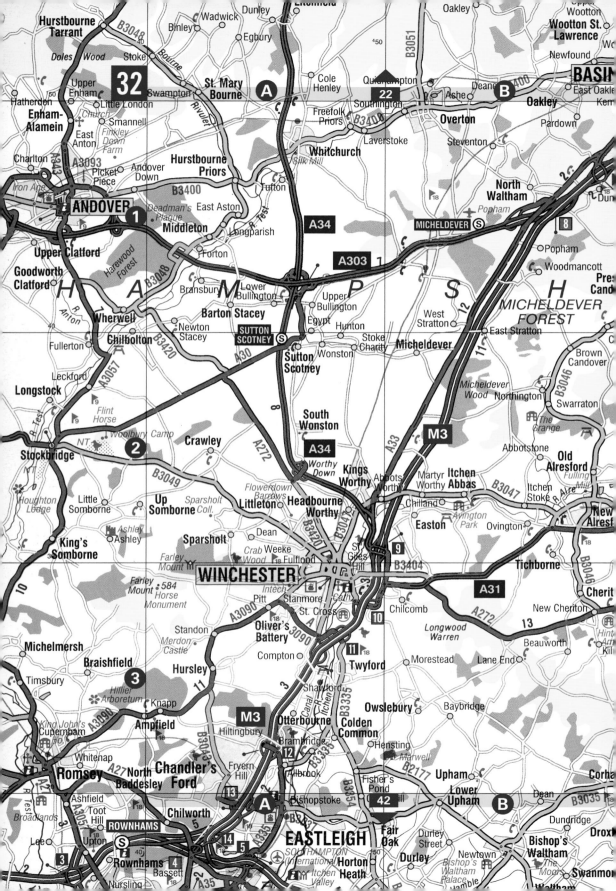

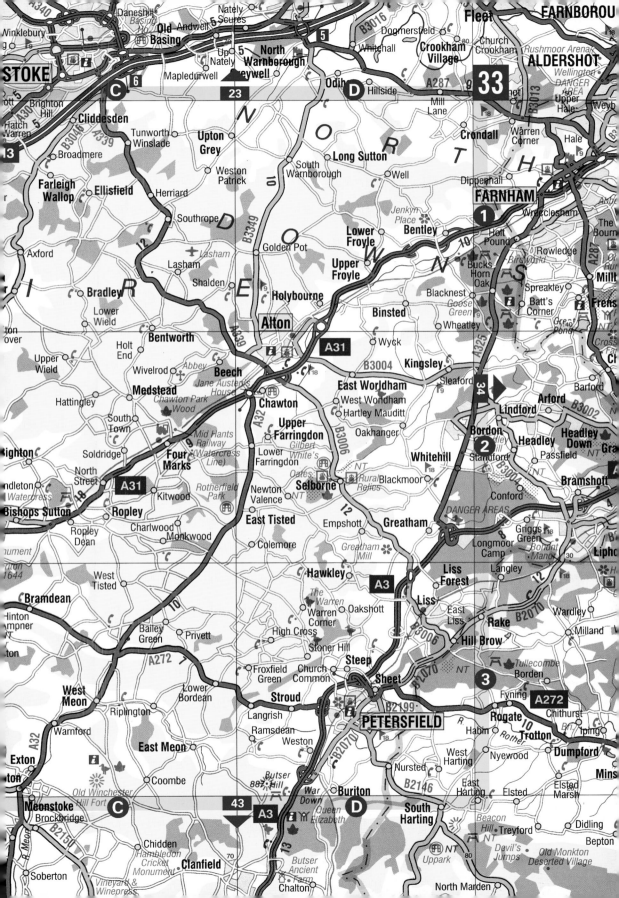

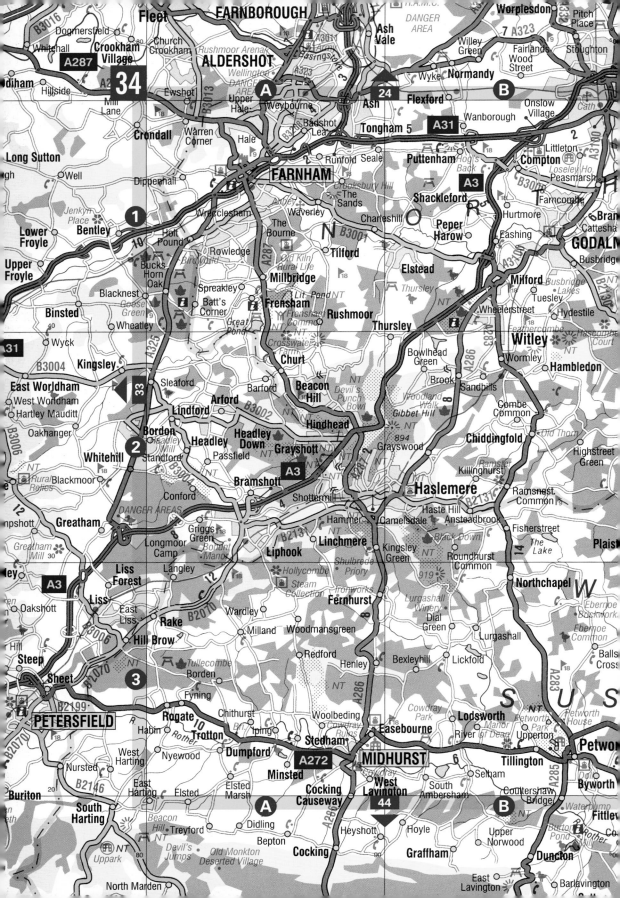

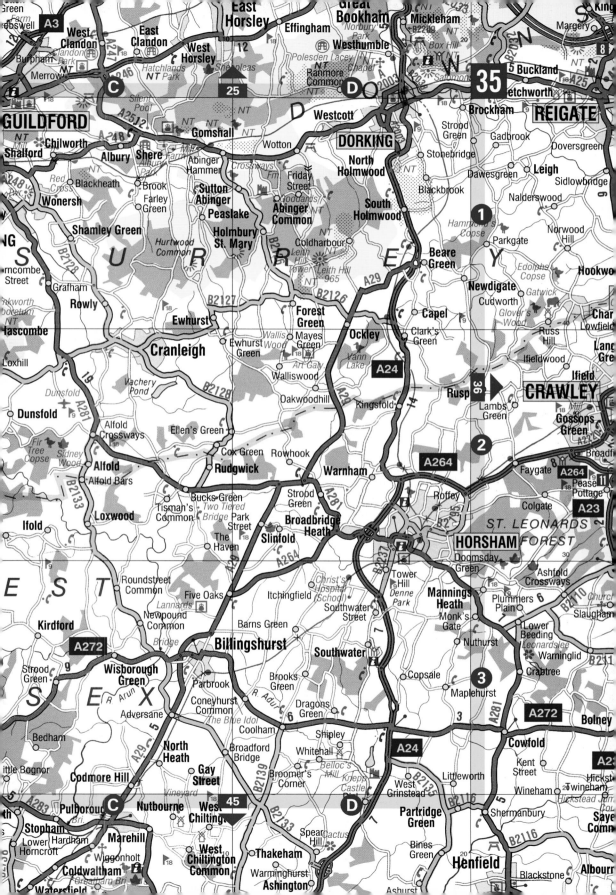

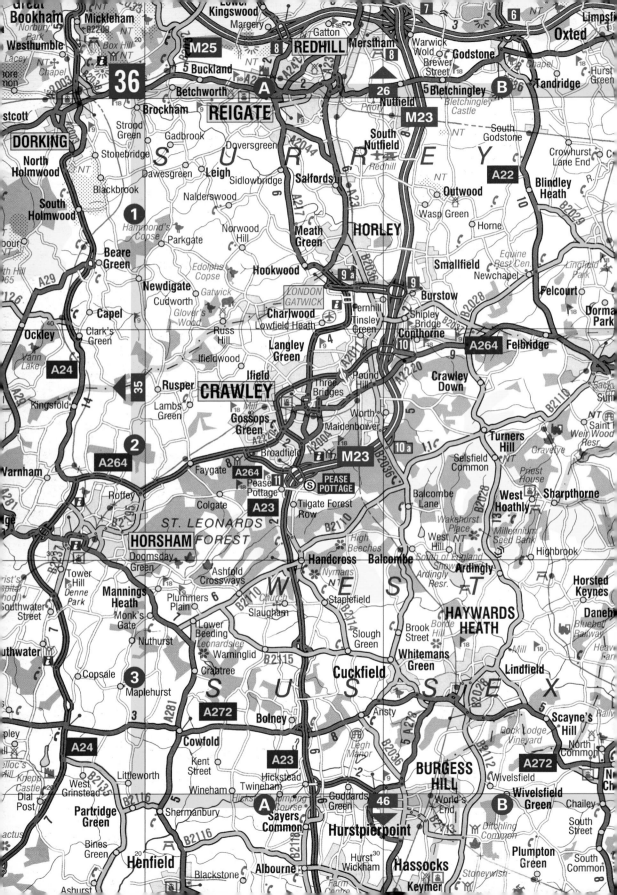

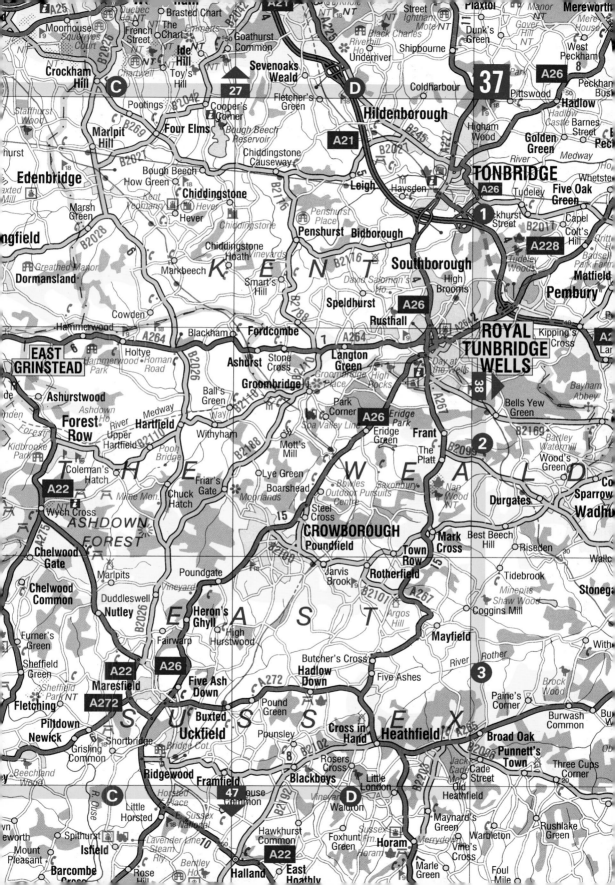

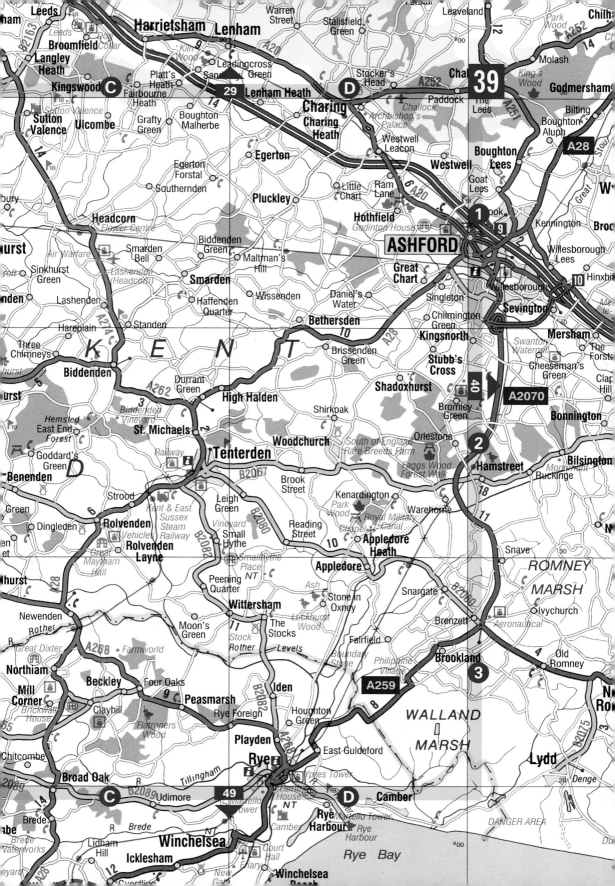

Portsmouth to:
Bilbao 30hrs.
Caen 6hrs. 15mins.
Cherbourg 5hrs.
Cherbourg 2hrs. 45mins.
 (Fast Ferry, Summer Only)
Le Havre 5hrs. 30mins.
St. Malo 8hrs. 45mins.

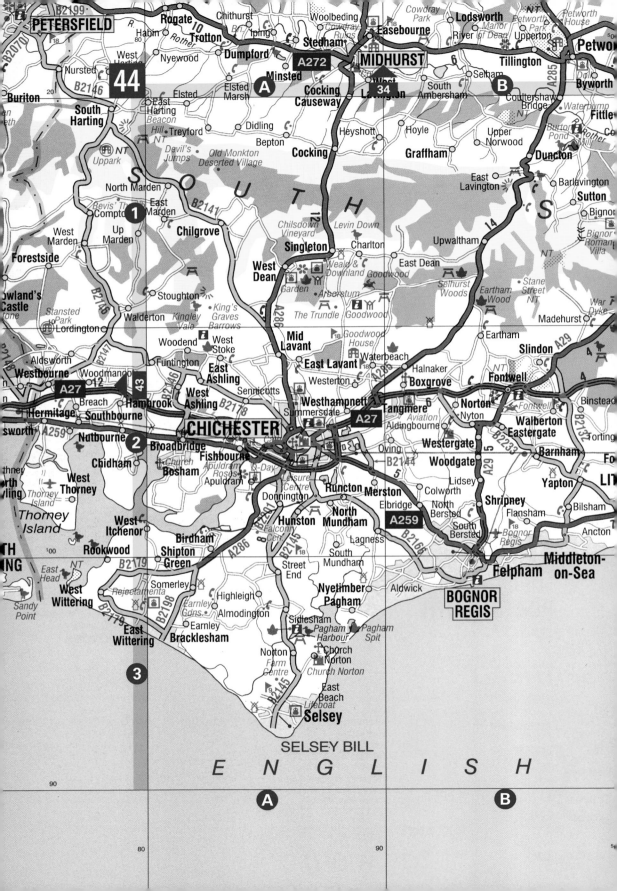

Mill
Corner
Brickwall
House
Clayhill
Peasmarsh
Rye Foreign
Houghton
Green
WALLAND
600
B2075
Chitcombe
Playden
A259
East Guldeford
MARSH
Lydd
49
Rye
39
Udimore
D
Camber
Broad
Oak
B2089
Brede
Winchelsea
NT
Rye
Harbour
Rye
Harbour
Martello Tower
DANGER AREA
Brede
Brede
Waterworks
Lidham
Hill
Icklesham
Court
Hall
Friary
Rye Bay
1
Westfield
Three Oaks
Guestling
Thorn
New
Gate
Winchelsea
Beach
Guestling
Wood
Pett
10
Baldslow
Guestling
Green
A259
The Mens
Cliff End
21
St.
Helen's
B2093
Fairlight
Cove
Caves
Ore
Fairlight
2
Hastings

HASTINGS
del
lage
ds

E   N   G   L   I   S   H

¹00

C   H   A   N   N   E   L

3

90

C
D
90
600

INDEX TO CITIES, TOWNS, VILLAGES, HAMLETS & LOCATIONS

(1) A strict alphabetical order is used e.g. Abbotstone follows Abbots Langley but precedes Abbots Worthy.

(2) The map reference given refers to the actual map square in which the town spot or built-up area is located and not to the place name.

(3) Where two places of the same name occur in the same County or Unitary Authority, the nearest large town is also given;
e.g. Ash. *Kent* —3C **31** (nr. Sandwich) indicates that Ash is located in square 3C on page **31** and is situated near Sandwich in the County of Kent.

COUNTIES AND UNITARY AUTHORITIES with the abbreviations used in this index.

Bedfordshire : *Beds*
Bracknell Forest : *Brac*
Brighton & Hove : *Brig*
Buckinghamshire : *Buck*
Cambridgeshire : *Cambs*
East Sussex : *E Sus*
Essex : *Essx*

Greater London : *G Lon*
Hampshire : *Hants*
Hertfordshire : *Herts*
Isle of Wight : *IOW*
Kent : *Kent*
Luton : *Lutn*
Medway : *Medw*

Milton Keynes : *Mil*
Northamptonshire : *Nptn*
Oxfordshire : *Oxon*
Portsmouth : *Port*
Reading : *Read*
Slough : *Slo*
Southampton : *Sotn*

Southend-on-Sea : *S'end*
Suffolk : *Suff*
Surrey : *Surr*
Thurrock : *Thur*
Warwickshire : *Warw*
West Berkshire : *W Ber*
West Sussex : *W Sus*

Windsor & Maidenhead :
Wind
Wokingham : *Wok*

Bexley. *G Lon* —1C **27**
Bexleyheath. *G Lon* —1C **27**
Bexleyhill. *W Sus* —3B **34**
Bicester. *Oxon* —2B **4**
Bicknacre. *Essx* —1B **20**
Bicknor. *Kent* —3C **29**
Bidborough. *Kent* —1D **37**
Biddenden. *Kent* —2C **39**
Biddenden Green. *Kent* —1C **39**
Biddlesden. *Buck* —1C **5**
Bierton. *Buck* —3A **6**
Biggin Hill. *G Lon* —3C **27**
Biggin Hill (London) Airport. *Kent* —2C **27**
Bighton. *Hants* —2C **33**
Bignor. *W Sus* —1B **44**
Billericay. *Essx* —2A **20**
Billingshurst. *W Sus* —3C **35**
Billington. *Beds* —2B **6**
Bilsham. *W Sus* —2B **44**
Bilsington. *Kent* —2A **40**
Bilting. *Kent* —1A **40**
Bines Green. *W Sus* —1D **45**
Binfield. *Brac* —1A **24**
Binfield Heath. *Oxon* —1D **23**
Binley. *Hants* —3A **22**
Binstead. *IOW* —3B **42**
Binstead. *W Sus* —2B **44**
Binsted. *Hants* —1D **33**
Birch. *Essx* —3D **11**
Birchanger. *Essx* —2D **9**
Birch Green. *Essx* —3D **11**
Birchington. *Kent* —2C **31**
Birchmoor Green. *Beds* —1B **6**
Birdbrook. *Essx* —1B **10**
Birdham. *W Sus* —2A **44**
Birds Green. *Essx* —1D **19**
Birling. *Kent* —2A **28**
Birling Gap. *E Sus* —3D **47**
Bisham. *Wind* —3A **16**
Bishopsbourne. *Kent* —3B **30**
Bishop's Green. *Essx* —3A **10**
Bishop's Green. *Hants* —2B **22**
Bishop's Stortford. *Herts* —2C **9**
Bishops Sutton. *Hants* —2C **33**
Bishopstoke. *Hants* —1A **42**
Bishopstone. *Buck* —3A **6**
Bishopstone. *E Sus* —2C **47**
Bishop's Waltham. *Hants* —1B **42**
Bisley. *Surr* —3B **24**
Bitterne. *Sotn* —1A **42**
Bix. *Oxon* —3D **15**
Blackboys. *E Sus* —3D **37**
Blackbrook. *Surr* —1D **35**
Blackditch. *Oxon* —1A **14**
Blackfen. *G Lon* —1C **27**
Blackfield. *Hants* —2A **42**
Blackham. *E Sus* —2C **37**
Blackheath. *Essx* —2A **12**
Blackheath. *G Lon* —1B **26**
Blackheath. *Surr* —1C **35**
Blackmoor. *Hants* —2D **33**
Blackmore. *Essx* —1A **20**
Blackmore End. *Essx* —1B **10**
Blackmore End. *Herts* —3D **7**
Blacknest. *Hants* —1D **33**
Black Notley. *Essx* —2B **10**
Blackstone. *W Sus* —1A **46**
Blackthorn. *Oxon* —3C **5**
Blackwater. *Hants* —3A **24**
Blackwater. *IOW* —3B **42**
Bladon. *Oxon* —3A **4**
Blake End. *Essx* —2B **10**
Blean. *Kent* —2B **30**
Bledlow. *Buck* —1D **15**
Bledlow Ridge. *Buck* —2D **15**
Blendworth. *Hants* —1D **43**
Blenheim. *Oxon* —1B **14**
Bletchingdon. *Oxon* —3B **4**
Bletchingley. *Surr* —3B **26**
Bletchley. *Mil* —1A **6**
Blewbury. *Oxon* —3B **14**
Blindley Heath. *Surr* —1B **36**
Bloxham. *Oxon* —1A **4**
Blue Bell Hill. *Kent* —2B **28**
Blue Row. *Essx* —3A **12**
Bluetown. *Kent* —3D **29**
Boarhunt. *Hants* —2C **43**
Boarshead. *E Sus* —2D **37**
Boars Hill. *Oxon* —1A **14**
Boarstall. *Buck* —3C **5**
Bobbing. *Kent* —2C **29**
Bobbingworth. *Essx* —1D **19**
Bocking. *Essx* —2B **10**
Bocking Churchstreet. *Essx* —2B **10**
Bodiam. *E Sus* —3B **38**
Bodicote. *Oxon* —1A **4**
Bodle Street Green. *E Sus* —1A **48**
Bodsham Green. *Kent* —1B **40**
Bognor Regis. *W Sus* —3B **44**
Bolney. *W Sus* —3A **36**
Bonnington. *Kent* —2A **40**
Booker. *Buck* —2A **16**
Boorley Green. *Hants* —1B **42**
Borden. *Kent* —2C **29**
Borden. *W Sus* —3A **34**
Bordon. *Hants* —2A **34**
Boreham. *Essx* —1B **20**
Boreham Street. *E Sus* —1A **48**
Borehamwood. *Herts* —2D **17**
Borley. *Essx* —1C **11**
Borley Green. *Essx* —1C **11**
Borough Green. *Kent* —3A **28**
Borstal. *Medw* —2B **28**
Bosham. *W Sus* —2A **44**
Bossingham. *Kent* —1B **40**
Botany Bay. *G Lon* —2A **18**
Bothampstead. *W Ber* —1B **22**
Botley. *Buck* —1B **16**
Botley. *Hants* —1B **42**
Botley. *Oxon* —1A **14**
Botolph Claydon. *Buck* —2D **5**
Botolphs. *W Sus* —2D **45**
Bough Beech. *Kent* —1C **37**
Boughton Aluph. *Kent* —1A **40**
Boughton Green. *Kent* —3B **28**
Boughton Lees. *Kent* —1A **40**
Boughton Malherbe. *Kent* —1C **39**
Boughton Monchelsea. *Kent* —3B **28**
Boughton under Blean. *Kent* —3A **30**
Bouldnor. *IOW* —3A **42**
Bourne End. *Buck* —3A **16**
Bourne End. *Herts* —1C **17**
Bournes Green. *S'end* —3D **21**
Bourne, The. *Surr* —1A **34**
Boveney. *Buck* —1B **24**
Bovingdon. *Herts* —1C **17**
Bovingdon Green. *Buck* —3A **16**
Bovinger. *Essx* —1D **19**
Bow Brickhill. *Mil* —1B **6**
Bowcombe. *IOW* —3A **42**
Bowers Gifford. *Essx* —3B **20**
Bowlhead Green. *Surr* —2B **34**
Boxford. *Suff* —1D **11**
Boxford. *W Ber* —1A **22**
Boxgrove. *W Sus* —2B **44**
Boxley. *Kent* —3B **28**
Boxted. *Essx* —1D **11**
Boxted Cross. *Essx* —1D **11**
Boyden Gate. *Kent* —2C **31**
Boyton Cross. *Essx* —1A **20**
Boyton End. *Essx* —1A **10**
Brabourne. *Kent* —1B **40**
Brabourne Lees. *Kent* —1A **40**
Bracklesham. *W Sus* —3A **44**
Brackley. *Nptn* —1B **4**
Brackley Hatch. *Nptn* —1C **5**
Bracknell. *Brac* —2A **24**
Bradenham. *Buck* —2A **16**
Bradfield. *Essx* —1B **12**
Bradfield. *W Ber* —1C **23**
Bradfield Heath. *Essx* —2B **12**
Brading. *IOW* —3C **43**
Bradley. *Hants* —1C **33**
Bradwell. *Essx* —2C **11**
Bradwell. *Mil* —1A **6**
Bradwell-on-Sea. *Essx* —3A **12**
Bradwell Waterside. *Essx* —1D **21**
Bragbury End. *Herts* —2A **8**
Braintree. *Essx* —2B **10**
Braishfield. *Hants* —3A **32**
Bramber. *W Sus* —1D **45**
Brambledown. *Kent* —1D **29**
Brambridge. *Hants* —3A **32**
Bramdean. *Hants* —3C **33**
Bramfield. *Herts* —3A **8**
Bramley. *Hants* —3C **23**
Bramley. *Surr* —1C **35**
Bramley Green. *Hants* —3C **23**
Bramling. *Kent* —3C **31**
Bramshill. *Hants* —2D **23**
Bramshott. *Hants* —2A **34**
Bran End. *Essx* —2A **10**
Bransbury. *Hants* —1A **32**
Brantham. *Suff* —1B **12**
Brasted. *Kent* —3C **27**
Brasted Chart. *Kent* —3C **27**
Braughing. *Herts* —2B **8**
Bray. *Wind* —1B **24**
Bray Wick. *Wind* —1A **24**
Breach. *W Sus* —2D **43**
Breachwood Green. *Herts* —2D **7**
Brede. *E Sus* —1C **49**
Bredgar. *Kent* —2C **29**
Bredhurst. *Kent* —2B **28**
Brenchley. *Kent* —1A **38**
Brent Cross. *G Lon* —3A **18**
Brentford. *G Lon* —1D **25**
Brent Pelham. *Herts* —1C **9**
Brentwood. *Essx* —2A **20**
Brenzett. *Kent* —3A **40**
Brewer Street. *Surr* —3B **26**
Bricket Wood. *Herts* —1D **17**
Bridge. *Kent* —3B **30**
Bridge Green. *Essx* —1C **9**
Bridgemary. *Hants* —2B **42**
Brighthampton. *Oxon* —1A **14**
Brightling. *E Sus* —3A **38**
Brightlingsea. *Essx* —3A **12**
Brighton. *Brig* —2B **46**
Brighton Hill. *Hants* —1C **33**
Brightwalton. *W Ber* —1A **22**
Brightwalton Green. *W Ber* —1A **22**
Brightwell. *Suff* —1C **13**
Brightwell Baldwin. *Oxon* —2C **15**
Brightwell-cum-Sotwell. *Oxon* —2B **14**
Brill. *Buck* —3C **5**
Brimpton. *W Ber* —2B **22**
Brissenden Green. *Kent* —2D **39**
Britwell Salome. *Oxon* —2C **15**
Brixton. *G Lon* —1B **26**
Broadbridge. *W Sus* —2A **44**
Broadbridge Heath. *W Sus* —2D **35**
Broadfield. *W Sus* —2A **36**
Broadford Bridge. *W Sus* —3C **35**
Broad Green. *Beds* —1B **6**
Broad Laying. *Hants* —2A **22**
Broadley Common. *Essx* —1C **19**
Broadmere. *Hants* —1C **33**
Broad Oak. *E Sus* —1C **49**
(nr. Hastings)
Broad Oak. *E Sus* —3A **38**
(nr. Heathfield)
Broadoak. *Hants* —1B **42**
Broad Oak. *Kent* —2B **30**
Broad's Green. *Essx* —3A **10**
Broadstairs. *Kent* —2D **31**
Broad Street. *Kent* —1B **40**
(nr. Ashford)
Broad Street. *Kent* —3C **29**
(nr. Maidstone)
Broad Street Green. *Essx* —1C **21**
Brockbridge. *Hants* —1C **43**
Brockham. *Surr* —1D **35**
Brockhurst. *Hants* —2C **43**
Brogborough. *Beds* —1B **6**
Bromley. *G Lon* —2C **27**
Bromley. *Herts* —2C **9**
Bromley Green. *Kent* —2D **39**
Brompton. *Medw* —2B **28**
Brook. *Hants* —3A **32**
Brook. *Kent* —1A **40**
Brook. *Surr* —1C **35**
(nr. Guildford)
Brook. *Surr* —2B **34**
(nr. Haslemere)
Brookland. *Kent* —3D **39**
Brookmans Park. *Herts* —1A **18**
Brooks Green. *W Sus* —3D **35**
Brook Street. *Essx* —2D **19**
Brook Street. *Kent* —2D **39**
Brook Street. *W Sus* —3B **36**
Brookwood. *Surr* —3B **24**
Broom. *Beds* —1D **7**
Broomer's Corner. *W Sus* —3D **35**
Broomfield. *Essx* —3B **10**
Broomfield. *Kent* —2B **30**
(nr. Herne Bay)
Broomfield. *Kent* —3C **29**
(nr. Maidstone)
Broomhall. *Surr* —2B **24**
Broughton. *Mil* —1A **6**
Broughton. *Oxon* —1A **4**
Brownbread Street. *E Sus* —1A **48**
Brown Candover. *Hants* —2B **32**
Broxbourne. *Herts* —1B **18**
Broxted. *Essx* —2D **9**
Broyle Side. *E Sus* —1C **47**
Bryant's Bottom. *Buck* —2A **16**
Buckhurst Hill. *Essx* —2C **19**
Buckingham. *Buck* —1C **5**
Buckland. *Buck* —3A **6**
Buckland. *Herts* —1B **8**
Buckland. *Kent* —1D **41**
Buckland. *Oxon* —2A **14**
Buckland. *Surr* —3A **26**
Buckland Common. *Buck* —1B **16**
Bucklebury. *W Ber* —1B **22**
Bucklers Hard. *Hants* —3A **42**
Bucklesham. *Suff* —1C **13**
Bucknell. *Oxon* —2B **4**
Bucks Green. *W Sus* —2C **35**
Bucks Hill. *Herts* —1C **17**
Bucks Horn Oak. *Hants* —1A **34**
Buffler's Holt. *Buck* —1C **5**
Bulbourne. *Herts* —3B **6**
Bull's Green. *Herts* —3A **8**
Bulmer. *Essx* —1C **11**
Bulmer Tye. *Essx* —1C **11**
Bulphan. *Thur* —3A **20**
Bulverhythe. *E Sus* —2B **48**
Bumble's Green. *Essx* —1C **19**
Buntingford. *Herts* —2B **8**
Buntings Green. *Essx* —1C **11**
Burchett's Green. *Wind* —3A **16**
Burcot. *Oxon* —2B **14**
Burcott. *Buck* —2A **6**
Burdrop. *Oxon* —1A **4**
Bures. *Suff* —1D **11**
Burgess Hill. *W Sus* —1B **46**
Burghclere. *Hants* —2A **22**
Burghfield. *W Ber* —2C **23**
Burghfield Common. *W Ber* —2C **23**
Burghfield Hill. *W Ber* —2C **23**
Burgh Heath. *Surr* —3A **26**
Burham. *Kent* —2B **28**
Buriton. *Hants* —3D **33**
Burleigh. *Brac* —1B **24**
Burmarsh. *Kent* —2B **40**
Burnham. *Buck* —3B **16**
Burnham Green. *Herts* —3A **8**
Burnham-on-Crouch. *Essx* —2D **21**
Burntcommon. *Surr* —3C **25**
Burnt Heath. *Essx* —2A **12**
Burnt Hill. *W Ber* —1B **22**
Burnt Oak. *G Lon* —2A **18**
Burpham. *Surr* —3C **25**
Burpham. *W Sus* —2C **45**
Burridge. *Hants* —1B **42**
Burrowhill. *Surr* —2B **24**
Bursledon. *Hants* —2A **42**
Burstow. *Surr* —1B **36**
Burton End. *Essx* —2D **9**
Burton's Green. *Essx* —2C **11**
Burwash. *E Sus* —3A **38**
Burwash Common. *E Sus* —3A **38**
Burwash Weald. *E Sus* —3A **38**
Bury. *W Sus* —1C **45**
Bury Green. *Herts* —2C **9**
Busbridge. *Surr* —1B **34**
Bushey. *Herts* —2D **17**
Bushey Heath. *Herts* —2D **17**
Bustard Green. *Essx* —2A **10**
Butcher's Cross. *E Sus* —3D **37**
Buttsash. *Hants* —2A **42**
Butt's Green. *Essx* —1B **20**
Buxted. *E Sus* —3C **37**
Bybrook. *Kent* —1A **40**
Byfleet. *Surr* —2C **25**
Bygrave. *Herts* —1A **8**
Byworth. *W Sus* —3B **34**

Caddington. *Beds* —3C **7**
Cade Street. *E Sus* —3A **38**
Cadmore End. *Buck* —2D **15**
Cadwell. *Herts* —1D **7**
Calais Street. *Suff* —1D **11**
Calbourne. *IOW* —3A **42**
Calcot Row. *W Ber* —1C **23**
Calcott. *Kent* —2B **30**
Caldecote. *Herts* —1A **8**
Caldecott. *Oxon* —2A **14**
Calshot. *Hants* —2A **42**
Calvert. *Buck* —2C **5**
Calverton. *Mil* —1D **5**
Camber. *E Sus* —1D **49**
Camberley. *Surr* —2A **24**
Camberwell. *G Lon* —1B **26**
Camden Town. *G Lon* —3A **18**
Camelsdale. *Surr* —2B **34**
Camps End. *Cambs* —1A **10**
Campton. *Beds* —1D **7**
Canadia. *E Sus* —1B **48**
Cane End. *Oxon* —1C **23**
Canewdon. *Essx* —2C **21**
Canterbury. *Kent* —3B **30**
Canvey Island. *Essx* —3B **20**
Capel. *Kent* —1A **38**
Capel. *Surr* —1D **35**
Capel-le-Ferne. *Kent* —2C **41**
Capel St Mary. *Suff* —1A **12**
Carisbrooke. *IOW* —3A **42**
Carshalton. *G Lon* —2A **26**
Cartbridge. *Surr* —3C **25**
Cassington. *Oxon* —3A **4**
Castle Camps. *Cambs* —1A **10**
Castle Green. *Surr* —2B **24**
Castle Hedingham. *Essx* —1B **10**
Castle Hill. *Kent* —1A **38**
Caterham. *Surr* —3B **26**
Catford. *G Lon* —1B **26**
Catherington. *Hants* —1C **43**
Catisfield. *Hants* —2B **42**
Catmore. *W Ber* —3A **14**
Catsfield. *E Sus* —1B **48**
Cattawade. *Suff* —1B **12**
Catteshall. *Surr* —1B **34**
Caulcott. *Oxon* —2B **4**
Caversfield. *Oxon* —2B **4**
Caversham. *Read* —1D **23**
Caversham Heights. *Read* —1C **23**
Chackmore. *Buck* —1C **5**

Chaddleworth. *W Ber* —1A **22**
Chadwell Heath. *G Lon* —3C **19**
Chadwell St Mary. *Thur* —1A **28**
Chafford Hundred. *Thur* —1A **28**
Chailey. *E Sus* —1B **46**
Chainhurst. *Kent* —1B **38**
Chaldon. *Surr* —3B **26**
Chalfont Common. *Buck* —2C **17**
Chalfont St Giles. *Buck* —2B **16**
Chalfont St Peter. *Buck* —3C **17**
Chalgrove. *Oxon* —2C **15**
Chalk. *Kent* —1A **28**
Chalk End. *Essx* —3A **10**
Challock. *Kent* —3A **30**
Chalton. *Beds* —2C **7**
Chalton. *Hants* —1D **43**
Chalvington. *E Sus* —2D **47**
Chandler's Cross. *Herts* —2C **17**
Chandler's Ford. *Hants* —3A **32**
Channel Tunnel. *Kent* —2B **40**
Chantry. *Suff* —1B **12**
Chapel End. *Beds* —1C **7**
Chapel Row. *W Ber* —1B **22**
Chapmore End. *Herts* —3B **8**
Chappel. *Essx* —2C **11**
Charing. *Kent* —1D **39**
Charing Heath. *Kent* —1D **39**
Charlbury. *Oxon* —3A **4**
Charleshill. *Surr* —1A **34**
Charlton. *G Lon* —1C **27**
Charlton. *Herts* —2D **7**
Charlton. *Nptn* —1B **4**
Charlton. *Oxon* —3A **14**
Charlton. *W Sus* —1A **44**
Charlton-on-Otmoor. *Oxon* —3B **4**
Charlwood. *Hants* —2C **33**
Charlwood. *Surr* —1A **36**
Charndon. *Buck* —2C **5**
Charney Bassett. *Oxon* —2A **14**
Chart Corner. *Kent* —3B **28**
Charter Alley. *Hants* —3B **22**
Chartham. *Kent* —3B **30**
Chartham Hatch. *Kent* —3B **30**
Chartridge. *Buck* —1B **16**
Chart Sutton. *Kent* —3B **28**
Chart, The. *Kent* —3C **27**
Charvil. *Wok* —1D **23**
Chatham. *Medw* —2B **28**
Chatham Green. *Essx* —3B **10**
Chattenden. *Medw* —1B **28**
Chattisham. *Suff* —1A **12**
Chaulden. *Herts* —1C **17**
Chaul End. *Beds* —2C **7**
Chawley. *Oxon* —1A **14**
Chawton. *Hants* —2D **33**
Cheam. *Surr* —2A **26**
Cheapside. *Wind* —2B **24**
Chearsley. *Buck* —3D **5**
Checkendon. *Oxon* —3C **15**
Cheddington. *Buck* —3B **6**
Cheeseman's Green. *Kent* —2A **40**
Chelmondiston. *Suff* —1C **13**
Chelmsford. *Essx* —1B **20**
Chelsea. *G Lon* —1A **26**
Chelsfield. *G Lon* —2C **27**
Chelsham. *Surr* —3B **26**
Chelwood Common. *E Sus* —3C **37**
Chelwood Gate. *E Sus* —3C **37**
Chenies. *Buck* —2C **17**
Cheriton. *Hants* —3B **32**
Cheriton. *Kent* —2C **41**
Cherry Green. *Herts* —2B **8**
Chertsey. *Surr* —2C **25**
Chesham. *Buck* —1B **16**
Chesham Bois. *Buck* —2B **16**
Cheshunt. *Herts* —1B **18**
Chessington. *G Lon* —2D **25**
Chesterton. *Oxon* —2B **4**
Chestfield. *Kent* —2B **30**
Chetwode. *Buck* —2C **5**
Chevening. *Kent* —3C **27**
Chichester. *W Sus* —2A **44**
Chidden. *Hants* —1C **43**
Chiddingfold. *Surr* —2B **34**
Chiddingly. *E Sus* —1D **47**
Chiddingstone. *Kent* —1C **37**
Chiddingstone Causeway. *Kent* —1D **37**
Chiddingstone Hoath. *Kent* —1C **37**
Chidham. *W Sus* —2D **43**
Chieveley. *W Ber* —1A **22**
Chignall St James. *Essx* —1A **20**
Chignall Smealy. *Essx* —3A **10**
Chigwell. *Essx* —2C **19**
Chigwell Row. *Essx* —2C **19**
Chilbolton. *Hants* —1A **32**
Chilcomb. *Hants* —3B **32**
Childrey. *Oxon* —3A **14**
Childwick Green. *Herts* —3D **7**
Chilgrove. *W Sus* —1A **44**
Chilham. *Kent* —3A **30**
Chilland. *Hants* —2B **32**
Chillenden. *Kent* —3C **31**
Chilmington Green. *Kent* —1D **39**
Chiltern Green. *Beds* —3D **7**
Chilton. *Buck* —3C **5**
Chilton. *Oxon* —3A **14**
Chilton Candover. *Hants* —1B **32**
Chilworth. *Hants* —1A **42**
Chilworth. *Surr* —1C **35**
Chimney. *Oxon* —1A **14**
Chineham. *Hants* —3C **23**
Chingford. *G Lon* —2B **18**
Chinnor. *Oxon* —1D **15**
Chipperfield. *Herts* —1C **17**
Chipping. *Herts* —1B **8**
Chipping Hill. *Essx* —3C **11**
Chipping Ongar. *Essx* —1D **19**
Chipstead. *Kent* —3D **27**
Chipstead. *Surr* —3A **26**
Chisbridge Cross. *Buck* —3A **16**
Chislehampton. *Oxon* —2B **14**
Chislehurst. *G Lon* —2C **27**
Chislet. *Kent* —2C **31**
Chiswell Green. *Herts* —1D **17**
Chiswick. *G Lon* —1A **26**
Chitcombe. *E Sus* —3C **39**
Chithurst. *W Sus* —3A **34**
Chobham. *Surr* —2B **24**
Cholesbury. *Buck* —1B **16**
Cholsey. *Oxon* —3B **14**
Chorleywood. *Herts* —2C **17**
Chrishall. *Essx* —1C **9**
Christmas Common. *Oxon* —2D **15**
Chuck Hatch. *E Sus* —2C **37**
Church Common. *Hants* —3D **33**
Church Crookham. *Hants* —3A **24**
Church End. *Beds* —2B **6** (nr. Dunstable)
Church End. *Beds* —1D **7** (nr. Stotfold)
Church End. *Beds* —1B **6** (nr. Woburn)
Church End. *Essx* —2B **10** (nr. Braintree)
Churchend. *Essx* —2A **10** (nr. Great Dunmow)
Church End. *Essx* —1D **9** (nr. Saffron Walden)
Churchend. *Essx* —2D **21** (nr. Southend)
Church End. *Hants* —3C **23**
Church Enstone. *Oxon* —2A **4**
Church Hanborough. *Oxon* —3A **4**
Church Hougham. *Kent* —1C **41**
Church Langley. *Essx* —1C **19**
Church Norton. *W Sus* —3A **44**
Church Street. *Kent* —1B **28**
Churt. *Surr* —2A **34**
Cippenham. *Slo* —3B **16**
City (London) Airport. *G Lon* —3C **19**
City of London. *G Lon* —3B **18**
City, The. *Buck* —2D **15**
Clacton-on-Sea. *Essx* —3B **12**
Clanfield. *Hants* —1C **43**
Clapgate. *Herts* —2C **9**
Clapham. *G Lon* —1A **26**
Clapham. *W Sus* —2C **45**
Clap Hill. *Kent* —2A **40**
Clark's Green. *Surr* —2D **35**
Clatterford. *IOW* —3A **42**
Clavering. *Essx* —1C **9**
Clay End. *Herts* —2B **8**
Claygate. *Kent* —1B **38**
Claygate. *Surr* —2D **25**
Claygate Cross. *Kent* —3A **28**
Clayhall. *Hants* —3C **43**
Clayhill. *E Sus* —3C **39**
Clayton. *W Sus* —1B **46**
Cleeve. *Oxon* —3C **15**
Cleveley. *Oxon* —2A **4**
Cliddesden. *Hants* —1C **33**
Cliffe. *Medw* —1B **28**
Cliff End. *E Sus* —1C **49**
Cliffe Woods. *Medw* —1B **28**
Cliffs End. *Kent* —2D **31**
Clifton. *Beds* —1D **7**
Clifton. *Oxon* —1A **4**
Clifton Hampden. *Oxon* —2B **14**
Cliftonville. *Kent* —1D **31**
Climping. *W Sus* —2B **44**
Clophill. *Beds* —1C **7**
Clothall. *Herts* —1A **8**
Coalhill. *Essx* —2B **20**
Coates. *W Sus* —1B **44**
Cobham. *Kent* —2A **28**
Cobham. *Surr* —2D **25**
Cock Clarks. *Essx* —1C **21**
Cockernhoe. *Herts* —2D **7**
Cockfosters. *G Lon* —2A **18**
Cock Green. *Essx* —3A **10**
Cocking. *W Sus* —1A **44**
Cocking Causeway. *W Sus* —1A **44**
Cockpole Green. *Wind* —3A **16**
Codicote. *Herts* —3A **8**
Codmore Hill. *W Sus* —3C **35**
Cogges. *Oxon* —1A **14**
Coggeshall. *Essx* —2C **11**
Coggeshall Hamlet. *Essx* —2C **11**
Coggins Mill. *E Sus* —3D **37**
Colchester. *Essx* —2A **12**
Cold Ash. *W Ber* —2B **22**
Coldean. *Brig* —2B **46**
Colden Common. *Hants* —3A **32**
Coldharbour. *Kent* —3D **27**
Coldharbour. *Surr* —1D **35**
Cold Norton. *Essx* —1C **21**
Coldred. *Kent* —1C **41**
Coldwaltham. *W Sus* —1C **45**
Cole Green. *Herts* —3A **8**
Cole Henley. *Hants* —3A **22**
Coleman Green. *Herts* —3D **7**
Coleman's Hatch. *E Sus* —2C **37**
Colemore. *Hants* —2D **33**
Coleshill. *Buck* —2B **16**
Colgate. *W Sus* —2A **36**
Collier Row. *G Lon* —2C **19**
Colliers End. *Herts* —2B **8**
Collier Street. *Kent* —1B **38**
Colnbrook. *Buck* —1C **25**
Colne Engaine. *Essx* —1C **11**
Colney Heath. *Herts* —1A **18**
Colney Street. *Herts* —1D **17**
Colt's Hill. *Kent* —1A **38**
Colworth. *W Sus* —2B **44**
Combe. *Oxon* —3A **4**
Combe. *W Ber* —2A **22**
Combe Common. *Surr* —2B **34**
Compton. *Hants* —3A **32**
Compton. *Surr* —1B **34**
Compton. *W Ber* —1B **22**
Compton. *W Sus* —1D **43**
Coneyhurst Common. *W Sus* —3D **35**
Conford. *Hants* —2A **34**
Conyer. *Kent* —2D **29**
Cooden. *E Sus* —2B **48**
Cookham. *Wind* —3A **16**
Cookham Dean. *Wind* —3A **16**
Cookham Rise. *Wind* —3A **16**
Cookley Green. *Oxon* —2C **15**
Cooksbridge. *E Sus* —1C **47**
Cooksmill Green. *Essx* —1A **20**
Coolham. *W Sus* —3D **35**
Cooling. *Medw* —1B **28**
Cooling Street. *Medw* —1B **28**
Coombe. *Hants* —3C **33**
Coombes. *W Sus* —2D **45**
Coopersale Common. *Essx* —1C **19**
Coopersale Street. *Essx* —1C **19**
Cooper's Corner. *Kent* —1C **37**
Cooper Street. *Kent* —3D **31**
Cootham. *W Sus* —1C **45**
Copdock. *Suff* —1B **12**
Copford. *Essx* —2D **11**
Copford Green. *Essx* —2D **11**
Copsale. *W Sus* —3D **35**
Copthall Green. *Essx* —1C **19**
Copthorne. *W Sus* —2B **36**
Corhampton. *Hants* —3C **33**
Cornish Hall End. *Essx* —1A **10**
Corringham. *Thur* —3B **20**
Coryton. *Thur* —3B **20**
Coscote. *Oxon* —3B **14**
Cosgrove. *Nptn* —1D **5**
Cosham. *Port* —2C **43**
Cote. *Oxon* —1A **14**
Cothill. *Oxon* —2A **14**
Cottered. *Herts* —2B **8**
Cottisford. *Oxon* —1B **4**
Coulsdon. *Surr* —3A **26**
Coultershaw Bridge. *W Sus* —1B **44**
Countess Cross. *Essx* —1C **11**
Court-at-Street. *Kent* —2A **40**
Courtsend. *Essx* —2D **21**
Cousley Wood. *E Sus* —2A **38**
Cove. *Hants* —3A **24**
Cowbeech. *E Sus* —1A **48**
Cowden. *Kent* —1C **37**
Cowes. *IOW* —3A **42**
Cowfold. *W Sus* —3A **36**
Cowley. *G Lon* —3C **17**
Cowley. *Oxon* —1B **14**
Cowplain. *Hants* —1C **43**
Cox Green. *Surr* —2C **35**
Coxheath. *Kent* —3B **28**
Crabtree. *W Sus* —3A **36**
Crafton. *Buck* —3A **6**
Cranbourne. *Brac* —1B **24**
Cranbrook. *Kent* —2B **38**
Cranbrook Common. *Kent* —2B **38**
Cranfield. *Beds* —1B **6**
Cranford. *G Lon* —1C **25**
Cranham. *G Lon* —3D **19**
Cranleigh. *Surr* —2C **35**
Cranmore. *IOW* —3A **42**
Crawley. *Hants* —2A **32**
Crawley. *W Sus* —2A **36**
Crawley Down. *W Sus* —2B **36**
Crayford. *G Lon* —1D **27**
Crays Hill. *Essx* —2B **20**
Cray's Pond. *Oxon* —3C **15**
Crazies Hill. *Wok* —3D **15**
Creekmouth. *G Lon* —3C **19**
Cressing. *Essx* —2B **10**
Crews Hill. *G Lon* —1B **18**
Cricket Hill. *Hants* —2A **24**
Cricklewood. *G Lon* —3A **18**
Cripp's Corner. *E Sus* —3B **38**
Crockenhill. *Kent* —2D **27**
Crocker End. *Oxon* —3D **15**
Crockerhill. *Hants* —2B **42**
Crockham Hill. *Kent* —3C **27**
Crockhurst Street. *Kent* —1A **38**
Crockleford Heath. *Essx* —2A **12**
Cromer. *Herts* —2A **8**
Crondall. *Hants* —1D **33**
Crookham. *W Ber* —2B **22**
Crookham Village. *Hants* —3D **23**
Cross-at-Hand. *Kent* —1B **38**
Cross Bush. *W Sus* —2C **45**
Cross End. *Essx* —1C **11**
Cross in Hand. *E Sus* —3D **37**
Crouch. *Kent* —3A **28**
Croughton. *Nptn* —1B **4**
Crowborough. *E Sus* —2D **37**
Crowdhill. *Hants* —1A **42**
Crowfield. *Nptn* —1C **5**
Crow Green. *Essx* —2D **19**
Crowhurst. *E Sus* —1B **48**
Crowhurst. *Surr* —1B **36**
Crowhurst Lane End. *Surr* —1B **36**
Crowmarsh Gifford. *Oxon* —3C **15**
Crowthorne. *Brac* —2A **24**
Croxley Green. *Herts* —2C **17**
Croydon. *G Lon* —2B **26**
Crundale. *Kent* —1A **40**
Crux Easton. *Hants* —3A **22**
Cryers Hill. *Buck* —2A **16**
Crystal Palace. *G Lon* —1B **26**
Cublington. *Buck* —2A **6**
Cuckfield. *W Sus* —3B **36**
Cuddesdon. *Oxon* —1C **15**
Cuddington. *Buck* —3D **5**
Cudham. *G Lon* —3C **27**
Cudworth. *Surr* —1A **36**
Cuffley. *Herts* —1B **18**
Culham. *Oxon* —2B **14**
Culverstone Green. *Kent* —2A **28**
Cumberlow Green. *Herts* —1B **8**
Cumnor. *Oxon* —1A **14**
Cupernham. *Hants* —3A **32**
Curbridge. *Hants* —1B **42**
Curdridge. *Hants* —1B **42**
Curridge. *W Ber* —1A **22**
Curtisden Green. *Kent* —1B **38**
Cutlers Green. *Essx* —1D **9**
Cuxham. *Oxon* —2C **15**
Cuxton. *Medw* —2B **28**

D

Dadford. *Buck* —1C **5**
Dagenham. *G Lon* —3C **19**
Dagnall. *Buck* —3B **6**
Dallington. *E Sus* —1A **48**
Danaway. *Kent* —2C **29**
Danbury. *Essx* —1B **20**
Dane End. *Herts* —2B **8**
Danehill. *E Sus* —3C **37**
Daneshill. *Hants* —3C **23**
Daniel's Water. *Kent* —1D **39**
Darenth. *Kent* —1D **27**
Dargate. *Kent* —2A **30**
Dartford. *Kent* —1D **27**
Dartford Crossing. *Kent* —1D **27**
Dassels. *Herts* —2B **8**
Datchet. *Wind* —1B **24**
Datchworth. *Herts* —3A **8**
Datchworth Green. *Herts* —3A **8**
Dawesgreen. *Surr* —1A **36**
Daws Heath. *Essx* —3C **21**
Deal. *Kent* —3D **31**
Dean. *Hants* —1B **42** (nr. Bishop's Waltham)
Dean. *Hants* —2A **32** (nr. Winchester)
Deane. *Hants* —3B **22**

Deanlane End. W Sus —1D 43
Deanshanger. Nptn —1D 5
Debden. Essx —1D 9
Debden Green. Essx —2C 19 (nr. Loughton)
Debden Green. Essx —1D 9 (nr. Saffron Walden)
Deddington. Oxon —1A 4
Dedham. Essx —1A 12
Dedham Heath. Essx —1A 12
Deepcut. Surr —3B 24
Delly End. Oxon —3A 4
Delvin End. Essx —1B 10
Denchworth. Oxon —2A 14
Dengie. Essx —1D 21
Denham. Buck —3C 17
Denham Green. Buck —3C 17
Denmead. Hants —1C 43
Densole. Kent —1C 41
Denstroude. Kent —2B 30
Denton. E Sus —2C 47
Denton. Kent —1C 41
Denton. Oxon —1B 14
Deptford. G Lon —1B 26
Derringstone. Kent —1C 41
Detling. Kent —3B 28
Dial Green. W Sus —3B 34
Dial Post. W Sus —1D 45
Dibden. Hants —2A 42
Dibden Purlieu. Hants —2A 42
Didcot. Oxon —2B 14
Didling. W Sus —1A 44
Digswell. Herts —3A 8
Dingleden. Kent —2C 39
Dinton. Buck —3D 5
Dipley. Hants —3D 23
Dippenhall. Surr —1A 34
Ditchling. E Sus —1B 46
Ditton. Kent —3B 28
Doddinghurst. Essx —2D 19
Doddington. Kent —3D 29
Dogmersfield. Hants —3D 23
Donkey Town. Surr —2B 24
Donnington. W Ber —2A 22
Donnington. W Sus —2A 44
Doomsday Green. W Sus —2D 35
Dorchester. Oxon —2B 14
Dorking. Surr —1D 35
Dorking Tye. Suff —1D 11
Dormansland. Surr —1C 37
Dormans Park. Surr —1B 36
Dorney. Buck —1B 24
Dorton. Buck —3C 5
Dover. Kent —1D 41
Dovercourt. Essx —1C 13
Doversgreen. Surr —1A 36
Dowlesgreen. Wok —2A 24
Downe. G Lon —2C 27
Downend. IOW —3B 42
Downend. W Ber —1A 22
Downham. Essx —2B 20
Downley. Buck —2A 16
Downside. Surr —3D 25
Dragons Green. W Sus —3D 35
Draycot. Oxon —1C 15
Drayton. Oxon —2A 14 (nr. Abingdon)
Drayton. Oxon —1A 4 (nr. Banbury)
Drayton. Port —2C 43
Drayton Beauchamp. Buck —3B 6
Drayton Parslow. Buck —2A 6
Drayton St Leonard. Oxon —2B 14
Drellingore. Kent —1C 41
Droxford. Hants —1C 43
Dry Sandford. Oxon —1A 14
Dry Street. Essx —3A 20
Duck End. Essx —2A 10
Ducklington. Oxon —1A 14
Duddenhoe End. Essx —1C 9
Dulwich. G Lon —1B 26
Dummer. Hants —1B 32
Dumpford. W Sus —3A 34
Duncton. W Sus —1B 44
Dundridge. Hants —1B 42
Dungate. Kent —3D 29
Dungeness. Kent —3A 40
Dunkirk. Kent —3A 30
Dunk's Green. Kent —3A 28
Dunley. Hants —3A 22
Dunsden Green. Oxon —1D 23
Dunsfold. Surr —2C 35
Dunsmore. Buck —1A 16
Dunstable. Beds —2C 7
Duns Tew. Oxon —2A 4
Dunton. Buck —2A 6
Dunton Green. Kent —3D 27
Durgates. E Sus —2A 38
Durley. Hants —1B 42
Durley Street. Hants —1B 42
Durrant Green. Kent —2C 39
Durrants. Hants —1D 43
Durrington. W Sus —2D 45
Duton Hill. Essx —2A 10
Duxford. Oxon —2A 14
Dymchurch. Kent —3B 40

Ealing. G Lon —3D 17
Earley. Wok —1D 23
Earls Colne. Essx —2C 11
Earnley. W Sus —3A 44
Eartham. W Sus —2B 44
Easebourne. W Sus —3A 34
Eashing. Surr —1B 34
Easington. Buck —3C 5
Easington. Oxon —1A 4 (nr. Banbury)
Easington. Oxon —2C 15 (nr. Watlington)
Easole Street. Kent —3C 31
East Anton. Hants —1A 32
East Ashling. W Sus —2A 44
East Aston. Hants —1A 32
East Barming. Kent —3B 28
East Barnet. G Lon —2A 18
East Beach. W Sus —3A 44
East Bedfont. G Lon —1C 25
East Bergholt. Suff —1A 12
East Blatchington. E Sus —3C 47
East Boldre. Hants —2A 42
Eastbourne. E Sus —3A 48
East Burnham. Buck —3B 16
Eastbury. Herts —2C 17
Eastbury. W Ber —1A 22
East Challow. Oxon —3A 14
East Chiltington. E Sus —1B 46
Eastchurch. Kent —1D 29
East Clandon. Surr —3C 25
East Claydon. Buck —2D 5
Eastcote. G Lon —3D 17
East Cowes. IOW —3B 42
East Dean. E Sus —3D 47
East Dean. W Sus —1B 44
East End. Hants —3A 42 (nr. Lymington)
East End. Hants —2A 22 (nr. Newbury)
East End. Herts —2C 9
East End. Kent —1D 29 (nr. Minster)
East End. Kent —2C 39 (nr. Tenterden)
East End. Oxon —3A 4
East End. Suff —1B 12
Eastergate. W Sus —2B 44
East Farleigh. Kent —3B 28
East Garston. W Ber —1A 22
East Ginge. Oxon —3A 14
East Gores. Essx —2C 11
East Grinstead. W Sus —2B 36
East Guldeford. E Sus —3D 39
East Hagbourne. Oxon —3B 14
East Ham. G Lon —3C 19
Easthampstead. Brac —2A 24
East Hanney. Oxon —2A 14
East Hanningfield. Essx —1B 20
East Harting. W Sus —1A 44
Eastheath. Wok —2A 24
East Hendred. Oxon —3A 14
East Hoathly. E Sus —1D 47
Easthorpe. Essx —2D 11
East Horsley. Surr —3C 25
East Hyde. Beds —3D 7
East Ilsley. W Ber —3A 14
East Langdon. Kent —1D 41
East Lavant. W Sus —2A 44
East Lavington. W Sus —1B 44
Eastleigh. Hants —1A 42
Eastling. Kent —3D 29
East Liss. Hants —3D 33
East Lockinge. Oxon —3A 14
East Malling. Kent —3B 28
East Marden. W Sus —1A 44
East Meon. Hants —3C 33
East Mersea. Essx —3A 12
East Molesey. Surr —2D 25
Eastney. Port —3C 43
East Oakley. Hants —3B 22
Easton. Hants —2B 32
East Peckham. Kent —1A 38
East Preston. W Sus —2C 45
Eastry. Kent —3D 31
East Shefford. W Ber —1A 22
East Stourmouth. Kent —2C 31
East Stratton. Hants —1B 32
East Studdal. Kent —1D 41
East Tilbury. Thur —1A 28
East Tisted. Hants —2D 33
Eastwick. Herts —3C 9
East Wittering. W Sus —3D 43
Eastwood. S'end —3C 21
East Woodhay. Hants —2A 22
East Worldham. Hants —2D 33
Eaton. Oxon —1A 14
Eaton Bray. Beds —2B 6
Eaton Green. Beds —2B 6
Ecchinswell. Hants —3B 22
Eccles. Kent —2B 28
Edburton. W Sus —1A 46
Eddington. W Ber —2A 22
Edenbridge. Kent —1C 37
Edgcott. Buck —2C 5
Edgware. G Lon —2D 17
Edlesborough. Buck —3B 6
Edmonton. G Lon —2B 18
Edney Common. Essx —1A 20
Edwardstone. Suff —1D 11
Edworth. Beds —1A 8
Effingham. Surr —3D 25
Effingham Common. Surr —3D 25
Egbury. Hants —3A 22
Egerton. Kent —1D 39
Egerton Forstal. Kent —1C 39
Eggington. Beds —2B 6
Egham. Surr —1C 25
Egypt. Buck —3B 16
Egypt. Hants —1A 32
Eight Ash Green. Essx —2D 11
Elbridge. W Sus —2B 44
Elcot. W Ber —1A 22
Elder Street. Essx —1D 9
Elham. Kent —1B 40
Eling. Hants —1A 42
Eling. W Ber —1B 22
Elkins Green. Essx —1A 20
Ellenbrook. Herts —1A 18
Ellen's Green. Surr —2C 35
Ellesborough. Buck —1A 16
Ellisfield. Hants —1C 33
Elmbridge. Surr —2C 35
Elmdon. Essx —1C 9
Elmfield. IOW —3B 42
Elm Park. G Lon —3D 19
Elmstead. Essx —2A 12
Elmstead Heath. Essx —2A 12
Elmstead Market. Essx —2A 12
Elmsted. Kent —1B 40
Elmstone. Kent —2C 31
Elsenham. Essx —2D 9
Elsfield. Oxon —3B 4
Elstead. Surr —1B 34
Elsted. W Sus —1A 44
Elsted Marsh. W Sus —3A 34
Elstree. Herts —2D 17
Eltham. G Lon —1C 27
Elvington. Kent —3C 31
Emmbrook. Wok —2D 23
Emmer Green. Read —1D 23
Emmington. Oxon —1D 15
Empshott. Hants —2D 33
Emsworth. Hants —2D 43
Enborne. W Ber —2A 22
Enborne Row. W Ber —2A 22
Enfield. G Lon —2B 18
Enfield Wash. G Lon —2B 18
Englefield. W Ber —1C 23
Englefield Green. Surr —1B 24
Enham Alamein. Hants —1A 32
Enstone. Oxon —2A 4
Epping. Essx —1C 19
Epping Green. Essx —1C 19
Epping Green. Herts —1A 18
Epping Upland. Essx —1C 19
Epsom. Surr —2A 26
Epwell. Oxon —1A 4
Eridge Green. E Sus —2D 37
Erith. G Lon —1D 27
Erriottwood. Kent —3D 29
Erwarton. Suff —1C 13
Esher. Surr —2D 25
Essendon. Herts —1A 18
Etchingham. E Sus —3B 38
Etchinghill. Kent —2B 40
Eton. Wind —1B 24
Eton Wick. Wind —1B 24
Evenley. Nptn —1B 4
Eversholt. Beds —1B 6
Eversley. Hants —2D 23
Eversley Cross. Hants —2D 23
Ewell. Surr —2A 26
Ewell Minnis. Kent —1C 41
Ewelme. Oxon —2C 15
Ewhurst. Surr —1C 35
Ewhurst Green. E Sus —3B 38
Ewhurst Green. Surr —2C 35
Ewshot. Hants —1A 34
Exbury. Hants —2A 42
Exceat. E Sus —3D 47
Exlade Street. Oxon —3C 15
Exton. Hants —3C 33
Eyhorne Street. Kent —3C 29
Eynsford. Kent —2D 27
Eynsham. Oxon —1A 14
Eythorne. Kent —1C 41

Faccombe. Hants —3A 22
Fairbourne Heath. Kent —3C 29
Fairfield. Kent —3D 39
Fairlands. Surr —3B 24
Fairlight. E Sus —1C 49
Fairlight Cove. E Sus —1C 49
Fairmile. Surr —2D 25
Fair Oak. Hants —1A 42 (nr. Eastleigh)
Fair Oak. Hants —2B 22 (nr. Kingsclere)
Fair Oak Green. Hants —2C 23
Fairseat. Kent —2A 28
Fairstead. Essx —3B 10
Fairwarp. E Sus —3C 37
Falkenham. Suff —1C 13
Falmer. E Sus —2B 46
Fancott. Beds —2C 7
Fanner's Green. Essx —3A 10
Fareham. Hants —2B 42
Farleigh. Surr —2B 26
Farleigh Wallop. Hants —1C 33
Farley Green. Surr —1C 35
Farley Hill. Wok —2D 23
Farlington. Port —2C 43
Farmoor. Oxon —1A 14
Farnborough. G Lon —2C 27
Farnborough. Hants —3A 24
Farnborough. W Ber —3A 14
Farncombe. Surr —1B 34
Farnham. Essx —2C 9
Farnham. Surr —1A 34
Farnham Common. Buck —3B 16
Farnham Green. Essx —2C 9
Farnham Royal. Buck —3B 16
Farningham. Kent —2D 27
Farthinghoe. Nptn —1B 4
Faulkbourne. Essx —3B 10
Faversham. Kent —2A 30
Fawkham Green. Kent —2D 27
Fawler. Oxon —3A 4
Fawley. Buck —3D 15
Fawley. Hants —2A 42
Fawley. W Ber —3A 14
Faygate. W Sus —2A 36
Feering. Essx —2C 11
Felbridge. Surr —2B 36
Felcourt. Surr —1B 36
Felden. Herts —1C 17
Felixstowe. Suff —1C 13
Felixstowe Ferry. Suff —1D 13
Felpham. W Sus —3B 44
Felsted. Essx —2A 10
Feltham. G Lon —1D 25
Felthamhill. G Lon —1C 25
Fencott. Oxon —3B 4
Fenn Street. Medw —1B 28
Fenny Stratford. Mil —1A 6
Fernhill. W Sus —1A 36
Fernhurst. W Sus —3A 34
Ferring. W Sus —2D 45
Fetcham. Surr —3D 25
Fewcott. Oxon —2B 4
Fiddlers Hamlet. Essx —1C 19
Fifield. Wind —1B 24
Finchampstead. Wok —2D 23
Finchdean. Hants —1D 43
Finchingfield. Essx —1A 10
Finchley. G Lon —2A 18
Findon. W Sus —2D 45
Findon Valley. W Sus —2D 45
Fingest. Buck —2D 15
Finglesham. Kent —3D 31
Fingringhoe. Essx —2A 12
Finmere. Oxon —1C 5
Finsbury. G Lon —3B 18
Finstock. Oxon —3A 4
Fishbourne. IOW —3B 42
Fishbourne. W Sus —2A 44
Fisher's Pond. Hants —3A 32
Fisherstreet. W Sus —2B 34
Fittleworth. W Sus —1C 45
Five Ash Down. E Sus —3C 37
Five Ashes. E Sus —3D 37
Five Oak Green. Kent —1A 38
Five Oaks. W Sus —3C 35
Flack's Green. Essx —3B 10
Flackwell Heath. Buck —3A 16
Flamstead. Herts —3C 7
Flansham. W Sus —2B 44
Flaunden. Herts —1C 17
Fleet. Hants —3A 24 (nr. Farnborough)
Fleet. Hants —2D 43 (nr. South Hayling)
Fleetville. Herts —1D 17
Fletcher's Green. Kent —1D 37
Fletching. E Sus —3C 37
Flexford. Surr —3B 24
Flimwell. E Sus —2B 38
Flishinghurst. Kent —2B 38
Flitton. Beds —1C 7
Flitwick. Beds —1C 7
Fobbing. Thur —3B 20
Folkestone. Kent —2C 41
Folkington. E Sus —2D 47
Folly, The. Herts —3D 7
Folly, The. W Ber —2A 22
Fontwell. W Sus —2B 44
Foots Cray. G Lon —1C 27
Ford. Buck —1D 15
Ford. W Sus —2C 45
Fordcombe. Kent —1D 37
Ford End. Essx —3A 10

Fordham. *Essx* —2D **11**
Fordham Heath. *Essx* —2D **11**
Ford Street. *Essx* —2D **11**
Fordwich. *Kent* —3B **30**
Forest Green. *Surr* —1D **35**
Forest Hill. *Oxon* —1B **14**
Forest Row. *E Sus* —2C **37**
Forestside. *W Sus* —1D **43**
Forstal, The. *Kent* —2A **40**
Forton. *Hants* —1A **32**
Forty Green. *Buck* —2B **16**
Forty Hill. *G Lon* —2B **18**
Foster Street. *Essx* —1C **19**
Foul Mile. *E Sus* —1A **48**
Four Elms. *Kent* —1C **37**
Four Marks. *Hants* —2C **33**
Four Oaks. *E Sus* —3C **39**
Four Throws. *Kent* —3B **38**
Foxcombe Hill. *Oxon* —1A **14**
Fox Corner. *Surr* —3B **24**
Fox Hatch. *Essx* —2D **19**
Foxhunt Green. *E Sus*
—1D **47**
Fox Lane. *Hants* —3A **24**
Fox Street. *Essx* —2A **12**
Framfield. *E Sus* —3C **37**
Frant. *E Sus* —2D **37**
Fratton. *Port* —2C **43**
Freefolk Priors. *Hants*
—1A **32**
Freeland. *Oxon* —3A **4**
French Street. *Kent* —3C **27**
Frensham. *Surr* —1A **34**
Freshwater. *IOW* —3A **42**
Freshwater Bay. *IOW* —3A **42**
Freston. *Suff* —1B **12**
Friar's Gate. *E Sus* —2C **37**
Friday Street. *E Sus* —2A **48**
Friday Street. *Surr* —1D **35**
Friern Barnet. *G Lon* —2A **18**
Frieth. *Buck* —2D **15**
Frilford. *Oxon* —2A **14**
Frilsham. *W Ber* —1B **22**
Frimley. *Surr* —3A **24**
Frimley Green. *Surr* —3A **24**
Frindsbury. *Medw* —2B **28**
Fringford. *Oxon* —2C **5**
Frinsted. *Kent* —3C **29**
Frinton-on-Sea. *Essx* —3C **13**
Friston. *E Sus* —3D **47**
Frithsden. *Herts* —3C **7**
Frittenden. *Kent* —1C **39**
Fritwell. *Oxon* —2B **4**
Frogham. *Kent* —3C **31**
Frogmore. *Hants* —2A **24**
Frogmore. *Herts* —1D **17**
Froxfield. *Beds* —1B **6**
Froxfield Green. *Hants*
—3D **33**
Fryern Hill. *Hants* —3A **32**
Fryerning. *Essx* —1A **20**
Fulflood. *Hants* —3A **32**
Fulham. *G Lon* —1A **26**
Fulking. *W Sus* —1A **46**
Fuller Street. *Essx* —3B **10**
Fullerton. *Hants* —2A **32**
Fulmer. *Buck* —3B **16**
Funtington. *W Sus* —2A **44**
Funtley. *Hants* —2B **42**
Furner's Green. *E Sus*
—3C **37**
Furneux Pelham. *Herts* —2C **9**
Furzeley Corner. *Hants*
—1C **43**
Furzey Lodge. *Hants* —2A **42**
Fyfield. *Essx* —1D **19**
Fyfield. *Oxon* —2A **14**
Fyning. *W Sus* —3A **34**

Gadbrook. *Surr* —1A **36**
Gagingwell. *Oxon* —2A **4**
Gainsborough. *Suff* —1B **12**
Gainsford End. *Essx* —1B **10**
Galleyend. *Essx* —1B **20**
Galleywood. *Essx* —1B **20**
Gallowstree Common. *Oxon*
—3C **15**
Gardeners Green. *Wok*
—2A **24**

Garford. *Oxon* —2A **14**
Garlinge Green. *Kent* —3B **30**
Garsington. *Oxon* —1B **14**
Gatton. *Surr* —3A **26**
Gatwick (London) Airport.
G Lon —1A **36**
Gawcott. *Buck* —1C **5**
Gay Bowers. *Essx* —1B **20**
Gay Street. *W Sus* —3C **35**
George Green. *Buck* —3B **16**
Gerrards Cross. *Buck* —3B **16**
Gestingthorpe. *Essx* —1C **11**
Gibralter. *Buck* —3D **5**
Gidea Park. *G Lon* —3D **19**
Gillingham. *Medw* —2B **28**
Gill's Green. *Kent* —2B **38**
Glassenbury. *Kent* —2B **38**
Glympton. *Oxon* —2A **4**
Glynde. *E Sus* —2C **47**
Glyndebourne. *E Sus* —1C **47**
Goathurst Common. *Kent*
—3C **27**
Goat Lees. *Kent* —1A **40**
Godalming. *Surr* —1B **34**
Goddard's Green. *Kent*
(nr. Benenden) —2C **39**
Goddard's Green. *Kent*
(nr. Cranbrook) —2B **38**
Goddards Green. *W Sus*
—3A **36**
Godmersham. *Kent* —3A **30**
Godstone. *Surr* —3B **26**
Goff's Oak. *Herts* —1B **18**
Golden Cross. *E Sus* —1D **47**
Golden Green. *Kent* —1A **38**
Golden Pot. *Hants* —1D **33**
Golders Green. *G Lon*
—3A **18**
Goldhanger. *Essx* —1D **21**
Goldstone. *Kent* —2C **31**
Gomshall. *Surr* —1C **35**
Good Easter. *Essx* —3A **10**
Goodmayes. *G Lon* —3C **19**
Goodnestone. *Kent* —3C **31**
(nr. Aylesham)
Goodnestone. *Kent* —2A **30**
(nr. Faversham)
Goodworth Clatford. *Hants*
—1A **32**
Goosey. *Oxon* —2A **14**
Goring. *Oxon* —3C **15**
Goring-by-Sea. *W Sus*
—2D **45**
Goring Heath. *Oxon* —1C **23**
Gosfield. *Essx* —2B **10**
Gosford. *Oxon* —3B **4**
Gosmore. *Herts* —2D **7**
Gosport. *Hants* —2B **42**
Gossops Green. *W Sus*
—2A **36**
Goudhurst. *Kent* —2B **38**
Graffham. *W Sus* —1B **44**
Grafham. *Surr* —1C **35**
Grafty Green. *Kent* —1C **39**
Grain. *Medw* —1C **29**
Granborough. *Buck* —2C **5**
Grandpont. *Oxon* —1B **14**
Grange Hill. *G Lon* —2C **19**
Graveley. *Herts* —2A **8**
Graveney. *Kent* —2A **30**
Gravesend. *Kent* —1A **28**
Grays. *Thur* —1A **28**
Grayshott. *Hants* —2A **34**
Grayswood. *Surr* —2B **34**
Grazeley. *Wok* —2C **23**
Great Amwell. *Herts* —3B **8**
Great Baddow. *Essx* —1B **20**
Great Bardfield. *Essx* —1A **10**
Great Bentley. *Essx* —2B **12**
Great Bookham. *Surr*
—3D **25**
Great Braxted. *Essx* —3C **11**
Great Brickhill. *Buck* —1B **6**
Great Bromley. *Essx* —2A **12**
Great Burstead. *Essx* —2A **20**
Great Canfield. *Essx* —3D **9**
Great Chart. *Kent* —1D **39**
Great Chesterford. *Essx*
—1D **9**
Great Chishill. *Cambs* —1C **9**
Great Clacton. *Essx* —3B **12**

Great Cornard. *Suff* —1C **11**
Great Dunmow. *Essx* —2A **10**
Great Easton. *Essx* —2A **10**
Great Gaddesden. *Herts*
—3C **7**
Great Hallingbury. *Essx*
—3D **9**
Greatham. *Hants* —2D **33**
Greatham. *W Sus* —1C **45**
Great Hampden. *Buck*
—1A **16**
Great Haseley. *Oxon* —1C **15**
Great Henny. *Essx* —1C **11**
Great Holland. *Essx* —3C **13**
Great Horkesley. *Essx*
—1D **11**
Great Hormead. *Herts* —1C **9**
Great Horwood. *Buck* —1D **5**
Great Kimble. *Buck* —1A **16**
Great Kingshill. *Buck* —2A **16**
Great Leighs. *Essx* —3B **10**
Great Linford. *Mil* —1A **6**
Great Maplestead. *Essx*
—1C **11**
Great Milton. *Oxon* —1C **15**
Great Missenden. *Buck*
—1A **16**
Great Mongeham. *Kent*
—3D **31**
Great Munden. *Herts* —2B **8**
Great Notley. *Essx* —2B **10**
Great Oakley. *Essx* —2B **12**
Great Offley. *Herts* —2D **7**
Great Oxney Green. *Essx*
—1A **20**
Great Parndon. *Essx* —1C **19**
Great Saling. *Essx* —2A **10**
Great Sampford. *Essx*
—1A **10**
Great Shefford. *W Ber*
—1A **22**
Great Stambridge. *Essx*
—2C **21**
Great Stonar. *Kent* —3D **31**
Greatstone-on-Sea. *Kent*
—3A **40**
Great Tew. *Oxon* —2A **4**
Great Tey. *Essx* —2C **11**
Great Thorness. *IOW* —3A **42**
Great Totham North. *Essx*
—3C **11**
Great Totham South. *Essx*
—3C **11**
Great Wakering. *Essx*
—3D **21**
Great Waldingfield. *Suff*
—1D **11**
Great Waltham. *Essx* —3A **10**
Great Warley. *Essx* —2D **19**
Great Wenham. *Suff* —1A **12**
Great Wigborough. *Essx*
—3D **11**
Greatworth. *Nptn* —1B **4**
Great Wymondley. *Herts*
—2A **8**
Great Yeldham. *Essx* —1B **10**
Green End. *Herts* —1B **8**
(nr. Buntingford)
Green End. *Herts* —2B **8**
(nr. Stevenage)
Greenfield. *Beds* —1C **7**
Greenfield. *Oxon* —2D **15**
Greenford. *G Lon* —3D **17**
Greenham. *W Ber* —2A **22**
Greenhill. *Kent* —2B **30**
Greenhithe. *Kent* —1D **27**
Greenstead Green. *Essx*
—2C **11**
Greensted Green. *Essx*
—1D **19**
Green Street. *Herts* —2D **17**
Green Street Green. *G Lon*
—2C **27**
Green Street Green. *Kent*
—1D **27**
Green Tye. *Herts* —3C **9**
Greenwich. *G Lon* —1B **26**
Grendon Underwood. *Buck*
—2C **5**
Greywell. *Hants* —3D **23**
Griggs Green. *Hants* —2A **34**

Grisling Common. *E Sus*
—3C **37**
Groombridge. *E Sus* —2D **37**
Groton. *Suff* —1D **11**
Grove. *Kent* —2C **31**
Grove. *Oxon* —2A **14**
Grove Park. *G Lon* —1B **26**
Gubblecote. *Herts* —3B **6**
Guestling Green. *E Sus*
—1C **49**
Guestling Thorn. *E Sus*
—1C **49**
Guildford. *Surr* —1B **34**
Gundleton. *Hants* —2C **33**
Gun Green. *Kent* —2B **38**
Gun Hill. *E Sus* —1D **47**
Gunville. *IOW* —3A **42**
Gurnard. *IOW* —3A **42**
Guston. *Kent* —1D **41**

Habin. *W Sus* —3A **34**
Hackney. *G Lon* —3B **18**
Haddenham. *Buck* —1D **15**
Hadham Cross. *Herts* —3C **9**
Hadham Ford. *Herts* —2C **9**
Hadleigh. *Essx* —3C **21**
Hadleigh. *Suff* —1A **12**
Hadleigh Heath. *Suff* —1D **11**
Hadley Wood. *G Lon* —2A **18**
Hadlow. *Kent* —1A **38**
Hadlow Down. *E Sus* —3D **37**
Haffenden Quarter. *Kent*
—1C **39**
Hailey. *Oxon* —3B **8**
Hailsham. *E Sus* —2D **47**
Hainault. *G Lon* —2C **19**
Hale. *Surr* —1A **34**
Hale Street. *Kent* —1A **38**
Halfway. *W Ber* —2A **22**
Halfway Houses. *Kent*
—1D **29**
Halland. *E Sus* —1D **47**
Halley. *Herts* —3B **8**
Halling. *Medw* —2B **28**
Hall's Green. *Herts* —2A **8**
Halnaker. *W Sus* —2B **44**
Halse. *Nptn* —1B **4**
Halstead. *Essx* —1C **11**
Halstead. *Kent* —2C **27**
Halton. *Buck* —1A **16**
Ham. *G Lon* —1D **25**
Ham. *Kent* —3D **31**
Hamble. *Hants* —2A **42**
Hambleden. *Buck* —3D **15**
Hambledon. *Hants* —1C **43**
Hambledon. *Surr* —2B **34**
Hambrook. *W Sus* —2D **43**
Ham Green. *Kent* —2C **29**
Ham Hill. *Kent* —2A **28**
Hammer. *W Sus* —2A **34**
Hammersmith. *G Lon* —1A **26**
Hammerwood. *E Sus* —2C **37**
Hammill. *Kent* —3C **31**
Hammond Street. *Herts*
—1B **18**
Hampden Park. *E Sus*
—2A **48**
Hamperden End. *Essx* —1D **9**
Hampstead. *G Lon* —3A **18**
Hampstead Norreys. *W Ber*
—1B **22**
Hampton. *G Lon* —1D **25**
Hampton. *Kent* —2B **30**
Hampton Poyle. *Oxon* —3B **4**
Hampton Wick. *G Lon*
—2D **25**
Hamsey. *E Sus* —1C **47**
Hamsey Green. *Surr* —3B **26**
Hamstead. *IOW* —3A **42**
Hamstead Marshall. *W Ber*
—2A **22**
Hamstreet. *Kent* —2A **40**
Handcross. *W Sus* —3A **36**
Handy Cross. *Buck* —2A **16**
Hangleton. *Brig* —2A **46**
Hangleton. *W Sus* —2C **45**
Hankham. *E Sus* —2A **48**
Hannington. *Hants* —3B **22**
Hanscombe End. *Beds* —1D **7**
Hanwell. *G Lon* —3D **17**

Hanwell. *Oxon* —1A **4**
Hanworth. *G Lon* —1D **25**
Harbledown. *Kent* —3B **30**
Hardham. *W Sus* —1C **45**
Hardley. *Hants* —2A **42**
Hardway. *Hants* —2C **43**
Hardwick. *Buck* —3A **6**
Hardwick. *Oxon* —2B **4**
(nr. Bicester)
Hardwick. *Oxon* —1A **14**
(nr. Witney)
Hardy's Green. *Essx* —2D **11**
Harefield. *G Lon* —2C **17**
Hare Green. *Essx* —2A **12**
Hare Hatch. *Wok* —1A **24**
Hareplain. *Kent* —2C **39**
Hare Street. *Essx* —1C **19**
Hare Street. *Herts* —2B **8**
Harkstead. *Suff* —1B **12**
Harlington. *Beds* —1C **7**
Harlington. *G Lon* —1C **25**
Harlow. *Essx* —1C **19**
Harmer Green. *Herts* —3A **8**
Harmondsworth. *G Lon*
—1C **25**
Harold Hill. *G Lon* —2D **19**
Harold Wood. *G Lon* —2D **19**
Harpenden. *Herts* —3D **7**
Harpsden. *Oxon* —3D **15**
Harrietsham. *Kent* —1A **40**
Harrow. *G Lon* —3D **17**
Harrow on the Hill. *G Lon*
—3D **17**
Harrow Weald. *G Lon*
—2D **17**
Hartfield. *E Sus* —2C **37**
Hartfordbridge. *Hants*
—3D **23**
Hartford End. *Essx* —3A **10**
Hartley. *Kent* —2B **38**
(nr. Cranbrook)
Hartley. *Kent* —2A **28**
(nr. Dartford)
Hartley Mauditt. *Hants*
—2D **33**
Hartley Wespall. *Hants*
—3C **23**
Hartley Wintney. *Hants*
—3D **23**
Hartlip. *Kent* —2C **29**
Harvel. *Kent* —2A **28**
Harwell. *Oxon* —3A **14**
Harwich. *Essx* —1C **13**
Hascombe. *Surr* —1B **34**
Haslemere. *Surr* —2B **34**
Hassell Street. *Kent* —1A **40**
Hassocks. *W Sus* —1B **46**
Haste Hill. *Surr* —2B **34**
Hastingleigh. *Kent* —1A **40**
Hastings. *E Sus* —2C **49**
Hastingwood. *Essx* —1C **19**
Hastoe. *Herts* —1B **16**
Hatch End. *G Lon* —2D **17**
Hatching Green. *Herts* —3D **7**
Hatch Warren. *Hants* —1C **33**
Hatfield. *Herts* —1A **18**
Hatfield Broad Oak. *Essx*
—3D **9**
Hatfield Heath. *Essx* —3D **9**
Hatfield Hyde. *Herts* —3A **8**
Hatfield Peverel. *Essx* —3B **10**
Hatford. *Oxon* —2A **14**
Hatherden. *Hants* —3A **22**
Hattingley. *Hants* —2C **33**
Hatton. *G Lon* —1C **25**
Haultwick. *Herts* —2B **8**
Havant. *Hants* —2D **43**
Havenstreet. *IOW* —3B **42**
Haven, The. *W Sus* —2C **35**
Havering-atte-Bower. *G Lon*
—2D **19**
Havering's Grove. *Essx*
—2A **20**
Haversham. *Mil* —1A **6**
Hawkenbury. *Kent* —1C **39**
Hawkhurst. *Kent* —2B **38**
Hawkhurst Common. *E Sus*
—1D **47**
Hawkinge. *Kent* —1C **41**
Hawkley. *Hants* —3D **33**
Hawkwell. *Essx* —2C **21**

Hawley. *Hants* —3A **24**
Hawley. *Kent* —1D **27**
Hawthorn Hill. *Brac* —1A **24**
Hayes. *G Lon* —2C **27**
(nr. Bromley)
Hayes. *G Lon* —3C **17**
(nr. Uxbridge)
Haylands. *IOW* —3B **42**
Haynes. *Beds* —1C **7**
Haynes West End. *Beds*
—1C **7**
Haysden. *Kent* —1D **37**
Hay Street. *Herts* —2B **8**
Haywards Heath. *W Sus*
—3B **36**
Hazeleigh. *Essx* —1C **21**
Hazeley. *Hants* —3D **23**
Hazel Street. *Kent* —2A **38**
Hazlemere. *Buck* —2A **16**
Headbourne Worthy. *Hants*
—2A **32**
Headcorn. *Kent* —1C **39**
Headington. *Oxon* —1B **14**
Headley. *Hants* —3A **34**
(nr. Haslemere)
Headley. *Hants* —2B **22**
(nr. Kingsclere)
Headley. *Surr* —3A **26**
Headley Down. *Hants* —2A **34**
Heath and Reach. *Beds*
—2B **6**
Heath Common. *W Sus*
—1D **45**
Heath End. *Hants* —2B **22**
Heathfield. *E Sus* —3D **37**
Heathrow (London) Airport.
G Lon —1C **25**
Heathton. *Suff* —1B **12**
Heaverham. *Kent* —3D **27**
Hebing End. *Herts* —2B **8**
Heckfield. *Hants* —2D **23**
Heckfordbridge. *Essx* —2D **11**
Hedge End. *Hants* —1A **42**
Hedgerley. *Buck* —3B **16**
Helions Bumpstead. *Essx*
—1A **10**
Hellingly. *E Sus* —1B **48**
Helmdon. *Nptn* —1B **4**
Hemel Hempstead. *Herts*
—1C **17**
Hemley. *Suff* —1C **13**
Hemp's Green. *Essx* —2D **11**
Hempstead. *Essx* —1A **10**
Hempstead. *Medw* —2B **28**
Hempton. *Oxon* —1A **4**
Hendon. *G Lon* —3A **18**
Henfield. *W Sus* —1A **46**
Henham. *Essx* —2D **9**
Henley. *W Sus* —3A **34**
Henley-on-Thames. *Oxon*
—3D **15**
Henley's Down. *E Sus*
—1B **48**
Henley Street. *Kent* —2A **28**
Henlow. *Beds* —1D **7**
Henny Street. *Essx* —1C **11**
Hensting. *Hants* —3A **32**
Henton. *Oxon* —1D **15**
Hermitage. *W Ber* —1B **22**
Hermitage. *W Sus* —2D **43**
Herne. *Kent* —2B **30**
Herne Bay. *Kent* —2B **30**
Herne Common. *Kent* —2B **30**
Herne Pound. *Kent* —3A **28**
Hernhill. *Kent* —2A **30**
Heronden. *Kent* —3C **31**
Herongate. *Essx* —2A **20**
Heronsgate. *Herts* —2C **17**
Heron's Ghyll. *E Sus* —3C **37**
Herriard. *Hants* —1C **33**
Hersden. *Kent* —2C **31**
Hersham. *Surr* —2C **25**
Herstmonceux. *E Sus* —1A **48**
Hertford. *Herts* —3B **8**
Hertford Heath. *Herts* —3B **8**
Hertingfordbury. *Herts* —3B **8**
Heston. *G Lon* —1D **25**
Hethe. *Oxon* —2B **4**
Hever. *Kent* —1C **37**
Hextable. *Kent* —1D **27**
Hexton. *Herts* —1D **7**

Heybridge. *Essx* —2A **20**
(nr. Brentwood)
Heybridge. *Essx* —1C **21**
(nr. Maldon)
Heybridge Basin. *Essx*
—1C **21**
Heydon. *Cambs* —1C **9**
Heyshott. *W Sus* —1A **44**
Heythrop. *Oxon* —2A **4**
Hickstead. *W Sus* —3A **36**
Higham. *Kent* —1B **28**
Higham. *Suff* —1A **12**
Higham Gobion. *Beds* —1D **7**
Higham Wood. *Kent* —1D **37**
High Barnet. *G Lon* —2A **18**
High Beech. *Essx* —2C **19**
Highbrook. *W Sus* —2B **36**
High Brooms. *Kent* —1D **37**
Highclere. *Hants* —2A **22**
High Cogges. *Oxon* —1A **14**
High Cross. *Hants* —3D **33**
High Cross. *Herts* —3B **8**
High Easter. *Essx* —3A **10**
High Garrett. *Essx* —2B **10**
Highgate. *G Lon* —3A **18**
High Halden. *Kent* —2C **39**
High Halstow. *Medw* —1B **28**
High Hurstwood. *E Sus*
—3C **37**
High Laver. *Essx* —1D **19**
Highleigh. *W Sus* —3A **44**
Highmoor. *Oxon* —3D **15**
High Ongar. *Essx* —1D **19**
High Roding. *Essx* —3A **10**
High Salvington. *W Sus*
—2D **45**
Highsted. *Kent* —2D **29**
Highstreet Green. *Essx*
—1B **10**
Highstreet Green. *Surr*
—2B **34**
High Wych. *Herts* —3C **9**
High Wycombe. *Buck* —2A **16**
Hildenborough. *Kent* —1D **37**
Hillborough. *Kent* —2C **31**
Hill Brow. *Hants* —3D **33**
Hillesden. *Buck* —2C **5**
Hill Green. *Essx* —1C **9**
Hillgreen. *W Ber* —1A **22**
Hill Head. *Hants* —2B **42**
Hillingdon. *G Lon* —3C **17**
Hillside. *Hants* —3D **23**
Hillstreet. *Hants* —1A **42**
Hill Top. *Hants* —2A **42**
Hilsea. *Port* —2C **43**
Hiltingbury. *Hants* —3A **32**
Hindhead. *Surr* —2A **34**
Hintlesham. *Suff* —1A **12**
Hinton Ampner. *Hants*
—3B **32**
Hinton-in-the-Hedges. *Nptn*
—1B **4**
Hinton Waldrist. *Oxon*
—2A **14**
Hinxhill. *Kent* —1A **40**
Hinxworth. *Herts* —1A **8**
Hipley. *Hants* —1C **43**
Hitchin. *Herts* —2D **7**
Hoaden. *Kent* —3C **31**
Hoath. *Kent* —2C **31**
Hobbs Cross. *Essx* —2C **19**
Hockley. *Essx* —2C **21**
Hockliffe. *Beds* —2B **6**
Hoddesdon. *Herts* —1B **18**
Hodsoll Street. *Kent* —2A **28**
Hoe Gate. *Hants* —1C **43**
Hogben's Hill. *Kent* —3A **30**
Hoggeston. *Buck* —2A **6**
Holborn. *G Lon* —3B **18**
Holbrook. *Suff* —1B **12**
Holbury. *Hants* —2A **42**
Holder's Green. *Essx* —2A **10**
Hole Street. *W Sus* —1D **45**
Holland-on-Sea. *Essx* —3B **12**
Hollingbourne. *Kent* —3C **29**
Hollingbury. *Brig* —2B **46**
Hollingdon. *Buck* —2A **6**
Hollingrove. *E Sus* —3A **38**
Hollington. *E Sus* —1B **48**
Holmbury St Mary. *Surr*
—1D **35**

Holmer Green. *Buck* —2A **16**
Holt End. *Hants* —2C **33**
Holton. *Oxon* —1C **15**
Holton St Mary. *Suff* —1A **12**
Holt Pound. *Hants* —1A **34**
Holtsmere End. *Herts* —3C **7**
Holtye. *E Sus* —2C **37**
Holwell. *Herts* —1D **7**
Holybourne. *Hants* —1D **33**
Holyfield. *Essx* —1B **18**
Holyport. *Wind* —1A **24**
Honey Hill. *Kent* —2B **30**
Honey Tye. *Suff* —1D **11**
Hooe. *E Sus* —2A **48**
Hooe Common. *E Sus*
—1A **48**
Hook. *G Lon* —2D **25**
Hook. *Hants* —3D **23**
(nr. Basingstoke)
Hook. *Hants* —2B **42**
(nr. Fareham)
Hook Green. *Kent* —2A **38**
(nr. Lamberhurst)
Hook Green. *Kent* —1A **28**
(nr. Longfield)
Hook Green. *Kent* —2A **28**
(nr. Meopham)
Hook Norton. *Oxon* —1A **4**
Hook's Cross. *Herts* —2A **8**
Hookwood. *Surr* —1A **36**
Hooley. *Surr* —3A **26**
Hoo St Werburgh. *Medw*
—1B **28**
Hope's Green. *Essx* —3B **20**
Horam. *E Sus* —1D **47**
Horkesley Heath. *Essx*
—2D **11**
Horley. *Oxon* —1A **4**
Horley. *Surr* —1A **36**
Hornchurch. *G Lon* —3D **19**
Horndean. *Hants* —1C **43**
Horndon on the Hill. *Thur*
—3A **20**
Horne. *Surr* —1B **36**
Horns Corner. *Kent* —3B **38**
Hornsey. *G Lon* —3B **18**
Horsell. *Surr* —3B **24**
Horsenden. *Buck* —1D **15**
Horsham. *W Sus* —2D **35**
Horsley Cross. *Essx* —2B **12**
Horsleycross Street. *Essx*
—2B **12**
Horsmonden. *Kent* —1A **38**
Horspath. *Oxon* —1B **14**
Horsted Keynes. *W Sus*
—3B **36**
Horton. *Buck* —3B **6**
Horton. *Wind* —1C **25**
Horton-cum-Studley. *Oxon*
—3B **4**
Horton Heath. *Hants* —1A **42**
Horton Kirby. *Kent* —2D **27**
Hothfield. *Kent* —1D **39**
Houghton. *Hants* —2A **32**
Houghton. *W Sus* —1C **45**
Houghton Conquest. *Beds*
—1C **7**
Houghton Green. *E Sus*
—3D **39**
Houghton Regis. *Beds*
—2C **7**
Hound. *Hants* —2A **42**
Hound Green. *Hants* —3D **23**
Hounslow. *G Lon* —1D **25**
Hounslow Green. *Essx*
—3A **10**
Hove. *Brig* —2A **46**
Howe Green. *Essx* —1B **20**
(nr. Chelmsford)
Howegreen. *Essx* —1C **21**
(nr. Maldon)
How End. *Beds* —1C **7**
Howe Street. *Essx* —3A **10**
(nr. Chelmsford)
Howe Street. *Essx* —1A **10**
(nr. Finchingfield)
How Green. *Kent* —1C **37**
Howlett End. *Essx* —1D **9**
Howt Green. *Kent* —2C **29**
Hoyle. *W Sus* —1B **44**
Hucking. *Kent* —3C **29**

Hughenden Valley. *Buck*
—2A **16**
Hulcott. *Buck* —3A **6**
Hullbridge. *Essx* —2C **21**
Hundred Acres. *Hants*
—1B **42**
Hungerford. *W Ber* —2A **22**
Hungerford Newtown. *W Ber*
—1A **22**
Hunny Hill. *IOW* —3A **42**
Hunsdon. *Herts* —3C **9**
Hunston. *W Sus* —2A **44**
Hunton. *Hants* —2A **32**
Hunton. *Kent* —1B **38**
Hunton Bridge. *Herts* —1C **17**
Hurley. *Wind* —3A **16**
Hursley. *Hants* —3A **32**
Hurst. *Wok* —1D **23**
Hurstbourne Priors. *Hants*
—1A **32**
Hurstbourne Tarrant. *Hants*
—3A **22**
Hurst Green. *E Sus* —3B **38**
Hurst Green. *Essx* —3A **12**
Hurst Green. *Surr* —3B **26**
Hurstpierpoint. *W Sus*
—1A **46**
Hurst Wickham. *W Sus*
—1A **46**
Hurtmore. *Surr* —1B **34**
Husborne Crawley. *Beds*
—1B **6**
Hutton. *Essx* —2A **20**
Hyde Heath. *Buck* —1B **16**
Hydestile. *Surr* —1B **34**
Hythe. *Hants* —2A **42**
Hythe. *Kent* —2B **40**
Hythe. *Surr* —1C **25**
Hythe End. *Wind* —1C **25**

Ibstone. *Buck* —2D **15**
Ibthorpe. *Hants* —3A **22**
Ibworth. *Hants* —3B **22**
Ickenham. *G Lon* —3C **17**
Ickford. *Buck* —1C **15**
Ickham. *Kent* —3C **31**
Ickleford. *Herts* —1D **7**
Icklesham. *E Sus* —1C **49**
Ide Hill. *Kent* —3C **27**
Iden. *E Sus* —3D **39**
Iden Green. *Kent* —2C **39**
(nr. Benenden)
Iden Green. *Kent* —2B **38**
(nr. Goudhurst)
Iffley. *Oxon* —1B **14**
Ifield. *W Sus* —2A **36**
Ifieldwood. *W Sus* —2A **36**
Ifold. *W Sus* —2C **35**
Iford. *E Sus* —2C **47**
Ightham. *Kent* —3D **27**
Ilford. *G Lon* —3C **19**
Ilmer. *Buck* —1D **15**
Ingatestone. *Essx* —2A **20**
Ingrave. *Essx* —2A **20**
Inkpen. *W Ber* —2A **22**
Inworth. *Essx* —3C **11**
Iping. *W Sus* —3A **34**
Ipsden. *Oxon* —3C **15**
Ipswich. *Suff* —1B **12**
Isfield. *E Sus* —1C **47**
Isle of Thanet. *Kent* —2D **31**
Isleworth. *G Lon* —1D **25**
Islington. *G Lon* —3B **18**
Islip. *Oxon* —3B **4**
Istead Rise. *Kent* —2A **28**
Itchen. *Sotn* —1A **42**
Itchen Abbas. *Hants* —2B **32**
Itchen Stoke. *Hants* —2B **32**
Itchingfield. *W Sus* —3D **35**
Iver. *Buck* —3C **17**
Iver Heath. *Buck* —3C **17**
Ivinghoe. *Buck* —3B **6**
Ivinghoe Aston. *Buck* —3B **6**
Ivychurch. *Kent* —3A **40**
Ivy Hatch. *Kent* —3D **27**
Iwade. *Kent* —2D **29**

Jacobswell. *Surr* —3B **24**
Jarvis Brook. *E Sus* —3D **37**
Jasper's Green. *Essx* —2B **10**

Jaywick. *Essx* —3B **12**
Jevington. *E Sus* —2D **47**
Jockey End. *Herts* —3C **7**
John's Cross. *E Sus* —3B **38**
Jordans. *Buck* —2B **16**

Kearsney. *Kent* —1C **41**
Kelshall. *Herts* —1B **8**
Kelvedon. *Essx* —3C **11**
Kelvedon Hatch. *Essx*
—2D **19**
Kempshott. *Hants* —3C **23**
Kemp Town. *Brig* —2B **46**
Kemsing. *Kent* —3D **27**
Kemsley. *Kent* —2D **29**
Kenardington. *Kent* —2D **39**
Kennington. *Kent* —1A **40**
Kennington. *Oxon* —1B **14**
Kensington. *G Lon* —1A **26**
Kensworth. *Beds* —3C **7**
Kensworth Common. *Beds*
—3C **7**
Kenton. *G Lon* —3D **17**
Kent Street. *E Sus* —1B **48**
Kent Street. *Kent* —3A **28**
Kent Street. *W Sus* —3A **36**
Kersey. *Suff* —1A **12**
Keston. *G Lon* —2C **27**
Kew. *G Lon* —1D **25**
Keymer. *W Sus* —1B **46**
Key Street. *Kent* —2C **29**
Kidbrooke. *G Lon* —1C **27**
Kiddington. *Oxon* —2A **4**
Kidlington. *Oxon* —3A **4**
Kidmore End. *Oxon* —1C **23**
Kilburn. *G Lon* —3A **18**
Killinghurst. *Surr* —2B **34**
Kilmeston. *Hants* —3B **32**
Kilndown. *Kent* —2B **38**
Kiln Green. *Wind* —1A **24**
Kimble Wick. *Buck* —1A **16**
Kimpton. *Herts* —3D **7**
Kingsash. *Buck* —1A **16**
Kingsbury. *G Lon* —3D **17**
Kingsclere. *Hants* —3B **22**
Kingsdown. *Kent* —1D **41**
Kingsey. *Buck* —1D **15**
Kingsfold. *W Sus* —2D **35**
Kingsgate. *Kent* —1D **31**
Kings Hill. *Kent* —3A **28**
Kings Langley. *Herts* —1C **17**
Kingsley. *Hants* —2D **33**
Kingsley Green. *W Sus*
—2A **34**
Kingsnorth. *Kent* —2A **40**
Kingsnorth. *Medw* —1C **29**
King's Somborne. *Hants*
—2A **32**
King's Sutton. *Nptn* —1A **4**
Kingston. *Kent* —3B **30**
Kingston. *W Sus* —2C **45**
Kingston Bagpuize. *Oxon*
—2A **14**
Kingston Blount. *Oxon*
—2D **15**
Kingston by Sea. *W Sus*
—2A **46**
Kingston near Lewes. *E Sus*
—2B **46**
Kingston Stert. *Oxon* —1D **15**
Kingston upon Thames.
G Lon —2D **25**
King's Walden. *Herts* —2D **7**
Kingswood. *Buck* —3C **5**
Kingswood. *Kent* —3C **29**
Kingswood. *Surr* —3A **26**
Kings Worthy. *Hants* —2A **32**
Kinsbourne Green. *Herts*
—3D **7**
Kintbury. *W Ber* —2A **22**
Kipping's Cross. *Kent* —1A **38**
Kirby Cross. *Essx* —2C **13**
Kirby le Soken. *Essx* —2C **13**
Kirdford. *W Sus* —3C **35**
Kirtlington. *Oxon* —3A **4**
Kirton. *Suff* —1C **13**
Kitwood. *Hants* —2C **33**
Knaphill. *Surr* —3B **24**
Knapp. *Hants* —3A **32**
Knatts Valley. *Kent* —2D **27**

Knebworth. *Herts* —2A **8**
Knockholt. *Kent* —3C **27**
Knockholt Pound. *Kent* —3C **27**
Knotty Green. *Buck* —2B **16**
Knowl Hill. *Wind* —1A **24**
Knowlton. *Kent* —3C **31**

Lacey Green. *Buck* —1A **16**
Laddingford. *Kent* —1A **38**
Lagness. *W Sus* —2A **44**
Laindon. *Essx* —3A **20**
Laleham. *Surr* —2C **25**
Lamarsh. *Essx* —1C **11**
Lamb Corner. *Essx* —1A **12**
Lamberhurst. *Kent* —2A **38**
Lamberhurst Quarter. *Kent* —2A **38**
Lambeth. *G Lon* —1B **26**
Lambourne End. *Essx* —2C **19**
Lambs Green. *W Sus* —2A **36**
Lancing. *W Sus* —2D **45**
Landport. *Port* —2C **43**
Lane End. *Buck* —2A **16**
Lane End. *Hants* —3B **32**
Lane End. *IOW* —3C **43**
Langdon Hills. *Essx* —3A **20**
Langdown. *Hants* —2A **42**
Langenhoe. *Essx* —3A **12**
Langford. *Beds* —1D **7**
Langford. *Essx* —1C **21**
Langham. *Essx* —1A **12**
Langley. *Essx* —1C **9**
Langley. *Hants* —2A **42**
Langley. *Herts* —2A **8**
Langley. *Kent* —3C **29**
Langley. *W Sus* —3A **34**
Langley. *Wind* —1C **25**
Langleybury. *Herts* —1C **17**
Langley Green. *W Sus* —2A **36**
Langley Heath. *Kent* —3C **29**
Langney. *E Sus* —2A **48**
Langrish. *Hants* —3D **33**
Langstone. *Hants* —2D **43**
Langton Green. *Kent* —2D **37**
Larkfield. *Kent* —3A **28**
Lasham. *Hants* —1C **33**
Lashenden. *Kent* —1C **39**
Latchford. *Herts* —2B **8**
Latchford. *Oxon* —1C **15**
Latchingdon. *Essx* —1C **21**
Latchmere Green. *Hants* —2C **23**
Latimer. *Buck* —2C **17**
Laughton. *E Sus* —1D **47**
Launton. *Oxon* —2C **5**
Laverstoke. *Hants* —1A **32**
Lawford. *Essx* —1A **12**
Layer Breton. *Essx* —3D **11**
Layer-de-la-Haye. *Essx* —2D **11**
Layer Marney. *Essx* —3D **11**
Layland's Green. *W Ber* —2A **22**
Layter's Green. *Buck* —2B **16**
Leaden Roding. *Essx* —3D **9**
Leadingcross Green. *Kent* —3C **29**
Leagrave. *Lutn* —2C **7**
Leatherhead. *Surr* —3D **25**
Leaveland. *Kent* —3A **30**
Leavenheath. *Suff* —1D **11**
Leaves Green. *G Lon* —2C **27**
Leckford. *Hants* —2A **32**
Leckhampstead. *Buck* —1D **5**
Leckhampstead. *W Ber* —1A **22**
Leckhampstead Street. *W Ber* —1A **22**
Ledburn. *Buck* —2B **6**
Ledwell. *Oxon* —2A **4**
Lee. *G Lon* —1C **27**
Lee. *Hants* —1A **42**
Lee Clump. *Buck* —1B **16**
Leeds. *Kent* —3C **29**
Lee-on-the-Solent. *Hants* —2B **42**
Lees, The. *Kent* —3A **30**
Lee, The. *Buck* —1B **16**
Leigh. *Kent* —1D **37**
Leigh. *Surr* —1A **36**
Leigh Beck. *Essx* —3C **21**
Leigh Green. *Kent* —2D **39**
Leigh-on-Sea. *S'end* —3C **21**
Leigh Park. *Hants* —2D **43**
Leighton Buzzard. *Beds* —2B **6**
Lemsford. *Herts* —3A **8**
Lenham. *Kent* —3C **29**
Lenham Heath. *Kent* —1D **39**
Lepe. *Hants* —3A **42**
Letchmore Heath. *Herts* —2D **17**
Letchworth. *Herts* —1A **8**
Letcombe Bassett. *Oxon* —3A **14**
Letcombe Regis. *Oxon* —3A **14**
Letty Green. *Herts* —3A **8**
Levens Green. *Herts* —2B **8**
Levington. *Suff* —1C **13**
Lewes. *E Sus* —1C **47**
Lewisham. *G Lon* —1B **26**
Lewknor. *Oxon* —2D **15**
Lewson Street. *Kent* —2D **29**
Leybourne. *Kent* —3A **28**
Ley Green. *Herts* —2D **7**
Ley Hill. *Buck* —1B **16**
Leysdown-on-Sea. *Kent* —1A **30**
Leyton. *G Lon* —3B **18**
Leytonstone. *G Lon* —3C **19**
Lickfold. *W Sus* —3B **34**
Lidham Hill. *E Sus* —1C **49**
Lidlington. *Beds* —1B **6**
Lidsey. *W Sus* —2B **44**
Lidstone. *Oxon* —2A **4**
Lightwater. *Surr* —2B **24**
Lilley. *Herts* —2D **7**
Lillingstone Dayrell. *Buck* —1D **5**
Lillingstone Lovell. *Buck* —1D **5**
Limbury. *Lutn* —2C **7**
Limpsfield. *Surr* —3B **26**
Linchmere. *W Sus* —2A **34**
Lindfield. *W Sus* —3B **36**
Lindford. *Hants* —2A **34**
Lindsell. *Essx* —2A **10**
Linford. *Thur* —1A **28**
Lingfield. *Surr* —1B **36**
Linkenholt. *Hants* —3A **22**
Linslade. *Beds* —2B **6**
Linton. *Kent* —3B **28**
Liphook. *Hants* —2A **34**
Lisle Court. *Hants* —3A **42**
Liss. *Hants* —3D **33**
Liss Forest. *Hants* —3D **33**
Litchfield. *Hants* —3A **22**
Litlington. *Cambs* —1B **8**
Litlington. *E Sus* —2D **47**
Little Baddow. *Essx* —1B **20**
Little Bardfield. *Essx* —1A **10**
Little Bentley. *Essx* —2B **12**
Little Billington. *Beds* —2B **6**
Little Bognor. *W Sus* —3C **35**
Little Bookham. *Surr* —3D **25**
Littlebourne. *Kent* —3C **31**
Little Brickhill. *Buck* —1B **6**
Little Bromley. *Essx* —2A **12**
Little Burstead. *Essx* —2A **20**
Littlebury. *Essx* —1D **9**
Littlebury Green. *Essx* —1C **9**
Little Canfield. *Essx* —2D **9**
Little Chalfont. *Buck* —2B **16**
Little Chart. *Kent* —1D **39**
Little Chesterford. *Essx* —1D **9**
Little Chishill. *Cambs* —1C **9**
Little Clacton. *Essx* —3B **12**
Little Common. *E Sus* —2B **48**
Little Cornard. *Suff* —1C **11**
Littlecote. *Buck* —2A **6**
Little Down. *Hants* —3A **22**
Little Dunmow. *Essx* —2A **10**
Little Easton. *Essx* —2A **10**
Little End. *Essx* —1D **19**
Little Gaddesden. *Herts* —3B **6**
Little Hadham. *Herts* —2C **9**
Little Hallingbury. *Essx* —3C **9**
Little Hampden. *Buck* —1A **16**
Littlehampton. *W Sus* —2C **45**
Little Haseley. *Oxon* —1C **15**
Little Horkesley. *Essx* —1D **11**
Little Hormead. *Herts* —2C **9**
Little Horsted. *E Sus* —1C **47**
Little Horwood. *Buck* —1D **5**
Little Kimble. *Buck* —1A **16**
Little Kingshill. *Buck* —2A **16**
Little Laver. *Essx* —1D **19**
Little Leighs. *Essx* —3B **10**
Little London. *Buck* —3C **5**
Little London. *E Sus* —1D **47**
Little London. *Hants* —1A **32**
(nr. Andover)
Little London. *Hants* —3C **23**
(nr. Basingstoke)
Little Maplestead. *Essx* —1C **11**
Little Marlow. *Buck* —3A **16**
Little Milton. *Oxon* —1C **15**
Little Missenden. *Buck* —2B **16**
Littlemore. *Oxon* —1B **14**
Little Oakley. *Essx* —2C **13**
Little Posbrook. *Hants* —2B **42**
Little Sampford. *Essx* —1A **10**
Little Sandhurst. *Brac* —2A **24**
Little Somborne. *Hants* —2A **32**
Littlestone-on-Sea. *Kent* —3A **40**
Little Tew. *Oxon* —2A **4**
Little Tey. *Essx* —2C **11**
Little Thurrock. *Thur* —1A **28**
Littleton. *G Lon* —2C **25**
Littleton. *Hants* —2A **32**
Littleton. *Surr* —1B **34**
Little Totham. *Essx* —3C **11**
Little Wakering. *Essx* —3D **21**
Little Walden. *Essx* —1D **9**
Little Waltham. *Essx* —3B **10**
Little Warley. *Essx* —2A **20**
Little Wenham. *Suff* —1A **12**
Littlewick Green. *Wind* —1A **24**
Little Wittenham. *Oxon* —2B **14**
Littleworth. *W Sus* —3D **35**
Little Wymondley. *Herts* —2A **8**
Little Yeldham. *Essx* —1B **10**
Littley Green. *Essx* —3A **10**
Locksgreen. *IOW* —3A **42**
Lock's Heath. *Hants* —2B **42**
Lodsworth. *W Sus* —3B **34**
London. *G Lon* —3B **18**
London Biggin Hill Airport. *Kent* —2C **27**
London City Airport. *G Lon* —3C **19**
London Colney. *Herts* —1D **17**
London Gatwick Airport. *W Sus* —1A **36**
London Heathrow Airport. *G Lon* —1C **25**
London Luton Airport. *Beds* —2D **7**
London Southend Airport. *Essx* —3C **21**
London Stansted Airport. *Essx* —2D **9**
Long Common. *Hants* —1B **42**
Long Crendon. *Buck* —1C **15**
Longcross. *Surr* —2B **24**
Long Ditton. *Surr* —2D **25**
Longfield. *Kent* —2A **28**
Longfield Hill. *Kent* —2A **28**
Longford. *G Lon* —1C **25**
Long Gardens. *Essx* —1C **11**
Long Hanborough. *Oxon* —3A **4**
Longlane. *W Ber* —1A **22**
Long Marston. *Herts* —3A **6**
Longmoor Camp. *Hants* —2D **33**
Longparish. *Hants* —1A **32**
Longstock. *Hants* —2A **32**
Long Sutton. *Hants* —1D **33**
Longwick. *Buck* —1D **15**
Long Wittenham. *Oxon* —2B **14**
Longworth. *Oxon* —2A **14**
Loose. *Kent* —3B **28**
Loosley Row. *Buck* —1A **16**
Lordington. *W Sus* —2D **43**
Loudwater. *Buck* —2B **16**
Loughton. *Essx* —2C **19**
Loughton. *Mil* —1A **6**
Lovedean. *Hants* —1C **43**
Loves Green. *Essx* —1A **20**
Lower Arncott. *Oxon* —3C **5**
Lower Assendon. *Oxon* —3D **15**
Lower Basildon. *W Ber* —1C **23**
Lower Beeding. *W Sus* —3A **36**
Lower Bordean. *Hants* —3C **33**
Lower Bullington. *Hants* —1A **32**
Lower Dicker. *E Sus* —1D **47**
Lower Farringdon. *Hants* —2D **33**
Lower Froyle. *Hants* —1D **33**
Lower Gravenhurst. *Beds* —1D **7**
Lower Green. *Essx* —1C **9**
Lower Green. *W Ber* —2A **22**
Lower Halstow. *Kent* —2C **29**
Lower Hardres. *Kent* —3B **30**
Lower Heyford. *Oxon* —2A **4**
Lower Higham. *Kent* —1B **28**
Lower Holbrook. *Suff* —1B **12**
Lower Horncroft. *W Sus* —1C **45**
Lower Horsebridge. *E Sus* —1D **47**
Lower Kingswood. *Surr* —3A **26**
Lower Layham. *Suff* —1A **12**
Lower Nazeing. *Essx* —1B **18**
Lower Rainham. *Medw* —2C **29**
Lower Raydon. *Suff* —1A **12**
Lower Shelton. *Beds* —1B **6**
Lower Shiplake. *Oxon* —1D **23**
Lower Stoke. *Medw* —1C **29**
Lower Sundon. *Beds* —2C **7**
Lower Swanwick. *Hants* —2A **42**
Lower Upham. *Hants* —1B **42**
Lower Upnor. *Medw* —1B **28**
Lower Wield. *Hants* —1C **33**
Lower Winchendon. *Buck* —3D **5**
Lower Woodend. *Buck* —3A **16**
Lowfield Heath. *W Sus* —1A **36**
Lowford. *Hants* —1A **42**
Loxhill. *Surr* —2C **35**
Loxwood. *W Sus* —2C **35**
Luddenham. *Kent* —2D **29**
Luddesdown. *Kent* —2A **28**
Ludgershall. *Buck* —3C **5**
Luffenhall. *Herts* —2A **8**
Lunsford. *Kent* —3B **28**
Lunsford's Cross. *E Sus* —1B **48**
Lurgashall. *W Sus* —3B **34**
Luton. *Lutn* —2C **7**
Luton. *Medw* —2B **28**
Luton (London) Airport. *Beds* —2D **7**
Lydd. *Kent* —3A **40**
Lydden. *Kent* —1C **41**
Lydd-on-Sea. *Kent* —3A **40**
Lyde Green. *Hants* —3D **23**
Lye Green. *Buck* —1B **16**
Lye Green. *E Sus* —2D **37**
Lyford. *Oxon* —2A **14**
Lymbridge Green. *Kent* —1B **40**
Lyminge. *Kent* —1B **40**
Lyminster. *W Sus* —2C **45**
Lympne. *Kent* —2B **40**
Lyne. *Surr* —2C **25**
Lynsted. *Kent* —2D **29**

Mackerye End. *Herts* —3D **7**
Madehurst. *W Sus* —1B **44**
Magdalen Laver. *Essx* —1D **19**
Magham Down. *E Sus* —1A **48**
Maidenbower. *W Sus* —2A **36**
Maidenhead. *Wind* —3A **16**
Maiden's Green. *Brac* —1A **24**
Maidensgrove. *Oxon* —3D **15**
Maid's Moreton. *Buck* —1D **5**
Maidstone. *Kent* —3B **28**
Maldon. *Essx* —1C **21**
Mallows Green. *Essx* —2C **9**
Maltman's Hill. *Kent* —1D **39**
Mannings Heath. *W Sus* —3A **36**
Manningtree. *Essx* —1B **12**
Manor Park. *G Lon* —3C **19**
Manston. *Kent* —2D **31**
Manuden. *Essx* —2C **9**
Maple Cross. *Herts* —2C **17**
Mapledurham. *Oxon* —1C **23**
Mapledurwell. *Hants* —3C **23**
Maplehurst. *W Sus* —3D **35**
Maplescombe. *Kent* —2D **27**
Marcham. *Oxon* —2A **14**
Marchwood. *Hants* —1A **42**
Marden. *Kent* —1B **38**
Marden Beech. *Kent* —1B **38**
Marden Thorn. *Kent* —1B **38**
Marehill. *W Sus* —1C **45**
Maresfield. *E Sus* —3C **37**
Margaret Roding. *Essx* —3D **9**
Margaretting. *Essx* —1A **20**
Margaretting Tye. *Essx* —1A **20**
Margate. *Kent* —1D **31**
Margery. *Surr* —3A **26**
Marine Town. *Kent* —1D **29**
Markbeech. *Kent* —1C **37**
Mark Cross. *E Sus* —2D **37**
Mark's Corner. *IOW* —3A **42**
Marks Tey. *Essx* —2D **11**
Markyate. *Herts* —3C **7**
Marle Green. *E Sus* —1D **47**
Marlow. *Buck* —3A **16**
Marlow Bottom. *Buck* —3A **16**
Marlpit Hill. *Kent* —1C **37**
Marlpits. *E Sus* —3C **37**
Marsh. *Buck* —1A **16**
Marshalswick. *Herts* —1D **17**
Marsh Baldon. *Oxon* —2B **14**
Marsh Benham. *W Ber* —2A **22**
Marshborough. *Kent* —3D **31**
Marsh Gibbon. *Buck* —2C **5**
Marsh Green. *Kent* —1C **37**
Marston. *Oxon* —1B **14**
Marston Moretaine. *Beds* —1B **6**
Marston St Lawrence. *Nptn* —1B **4**
Marsworth. *Buck* —3B **6**
Martin. *Kent* —1D **41**
Martin Mill. *Kent* —1D **41**
Martyr's Green. *Surr* —3C **25**
Martyr Worthy. *Hants* —2B **32**
Marylebone. *G Lon* —3A **18**
Mashbury. *Essx* —3A **10**
Matching. *Essx* —3D **9**
Matching Green. *Essx* —3D **9**
Matching Tye. *Essx* —3D **9**
Matfield. *Kent* —1A **38**
Mattingley. *Hants* —3D **23**
Maulden. *Beds* —1C **7**
Maxton. *Kent* —1D **41**

Maybush. Sotn —1A 42
Mayes Green. Surr —2D 35
Mayfield. E Sus —3D 37
Mayford. Surr —3B 24
Mayland. Essx —1D 21
Maylandsea. Essx —1D 21
Maynard's Green. E Sus —1D 47
Maypole. Kent —2C 31
Meadle. Buck —1A 16
Meath Green. Surr —1A 36
Medmenham. Buck —3A 16
Medstead. Hants —2C 33
Medway Towns. Medw —2B 28
Meesden. Herts —1C 9
Mentmore. Buck —3B 6
Meonstoke. Hants —1C 43
Meopham. Kent —2A 28
Meopham Green. Kent —2A 28
Meopham Station. Kent —2A 28
Meppershall. Beds —1D 7
Mereworth. Kent —3A 28
Merrow. Surr —3C 25
Mersham. Kent —2A 40
Merstham. Surr —3A 26
Merston. W Sus —2A 44
Merton. G Lon —2A 26
Merton. Oxon —3B 4
Messing. Essx —3C 11
Micheldever. Hants —2B 32
Michelmersh. Hants —3A 32
Mickleﬁeld Green. Herts —2C 17
Mickleham. Surr —3D 25
Middle Assendon. Oxon —3D 15
Middle Aston. Oxon —2A 4
Middle Barton. Oxon —2A 4
Middle Claydon. Buck —2D 5
Middleton. Essx —1C 11
Middleton. Hants —1A 32
Middleton Cheney. Nptn —1B 4
Middleton-on-Sea. W Sus —2B 44
Middleton Stoney. Oxon —2B 4
Middle Tysoe. Warw —1A 4
Midgham. W Ber —2B 22
Midhurst. W Sus —3A 34
Mid Lavant. W Sus —2A 44
Milcombe. Oxon —1A 4
Milebush. Kent —1B 38
Mile End. Essx —2D 11
Mile Oak. Brig —2A 46
Mile Town. Kent —1D 29
Milford. Surr —1B 34
Milland. W Sus —3A 34
Millbridge. Surr —1A 34
Millbrook. Beds —1C 7
Millbrook. Sotn —1A 42
Mill Corner. E Sus —3C 39
Mill End. Buck —3D 15
Mill End. Herts —1B 8
Mill Green. Suff —1D 11
Mill Greep. Essx —1A 20
Mill Hill. G Lon —2A 18
Mill Lane. Hants —3D 23
Millow. Beds —1A 8
Milstead. Kent —3D 29
Milton. Oxon —1A 4
(nr. Banbury)
Milton. Oxon —2A 14
(nr. Didcot)
Milton. Port —3C 43
Milton Bryan. Beds —1B 6
Milton Hill. Oxon —2A 14
Milton Keynes. Mil —1A 6
Milton Keynes Village. Mil —1A 6
Milton Regis. Kent —2C 29
Milton Street. E Sus —2D 47
Mimbridge. Surr —2B 24
Minsted. W Sus —3A 34
Minster. Kent —2D 31
(nr. Ramsgate)
Minster. Kent —1D 29
(nr. Sheerness)
Mistley. Essx —1B 12
Mistley Heath. Essx —1B 12
Mitcham. G Lon —2A 26
Mixbury. Oxon —1C 5
Molash. Kent —3A 30
Molehill Green. Essx —2D 9
Moneyrow Green. Wind —1A 24
Monken Hadley. G Lon —2A 18
Monk's Gate. W Sus —3A 36
Monk Sherborne. Hants —3C 23
Monks Risborough. Buck —1A 16
Monk Street. Essx —2A 10
Monkton. Kent —2C 31
Monkwood. Hants —2C 33
Moon's Green. Kent —3C 39
Moorgreen. Hants —1A 42
Moorhouse. Surr —3C 27
Moor, The. Kent —3B 38
Morden. G Lon —2A 26
Morestead. Hants —3B 32
Moreton. Essx —1D 19
Moreton. Oxon —1C 15
Morris Green. Essx —1B 10
Mortimer Common. W Ber —2C 23
Mortimer West End. Hants —2C 23
Mottingham. G Lon —1C 27
Mott's Mill. E Sus —2D 37
Moulsecoomb. Brig —2B 46
Moulsford. Oxon —3B 14
Moulsoe. Mil —1B 6
Mount Bures. Essx —1D 11
Mountfield. E Sus —3B 38
Mountnessing. Essx —2A 20
Mount Pleasant. Buck —1C 5
Mount Pleasant. E Sus —1C 47
Much Hadham. Herts —3C 9
Mucking. Thur —3A 20
Mugswell. Surr —3A 26
Mundon. Essx —1C 21
Murcott. Oxon —3B 4
Murrell Green. Hants —3D 23
Mursley. Buck —2A 6
Muswell Hill. G Lon —3A 18
Mytchett. Surr —3A 24

Nackington. Kent —3B 30
Nacton. Suff —1C 13
Nalderswood. Surr —1A 36
Naphill. Buck —2A 16
Nash. Buck —1D 5
Nash. Kent —3C 31
Nash Lee. Buck —1A 16
Nasty. Herts —2B 8
Nately Scures. Hants —3D 23
Navestock Heath. Essx —2D 19
Navestock Side. Essx —2D 19
Nayland. Suff —1D 11
Nazeing. Essx —1C 19
Neasden. G Lon —3A 18
Neithrop. Oxon —1A 4
Nethercott. Oxon —2A 4
Netherfield. E Sus —1B 48
Nether Street. Essx —3D 9
Netherton. Hants —3A 22
Nether Worton. Oxon —1A 4
Netley Abbey. Hants —2A 42
Nettlebed. Oxon —3D 15
Nettleden. Herts —3C 7
Nettlestead. Kent —3A 28
Nettlestead Green. Kent —3A 28
Nettlestone. IOW —3C 43
Nevendon. Essx —2B 20
New Addington. G Lon —2B 26
New Alresford. Hants —2B 32
New Ash Green. Kent —2A 28
New Barn. Kent —2A 28
Newbottle. Nptn —1B 4
Newbourne. Suff —1C 13
Newbridge. IOW —3A 42
New Brighton. Hants —2D 43
Newbury. W Ber —2A 22
Newchapel. Surr —1B 36
New Cheriton. Hants —3B 32
Newchurch. Kent —2A 40
New Denham. Buck —3C 17
Newdigate. Surr —1D 35
Newell Green. Brac —1A 24
New Eltham. G Lon —1C 27
Newenden. Kent —3C 39
New England. Essx —1B 10
Newfound. Hants —3B 22
Newgate Street. Herts —1B 18
New Greens. Herts —1D 17
Newhaven. E Sus —2C 47
New Haw. Surr —2C 25
New Hythe. Kent —3B 28
Newick. E Sus —3C 37
Newington. Kent —2B 40
(nr. Folkestone)
Newington. Kent —2C 29
(nr. Sittingbourne)
Newington. Oxon —2C 15
Newlands. Essx —3C 21
New Malden. G Lon —2A 26
Newman's Green. Suff —1C 11
New Mill. Herts —3B 6
New Mistley. Essx —1B 12
Newnham. Hants —3D 23
Newnham. Herts —1A 8
Newnham. Kent —3D 29
Newport. Essx —1D 9
Newport. IOW —3B 42
Newpound Common. W Sus —3C 35
New Romney. Kent —3A 40
Newton. Suff —1D 11
Newton Longville. Buck —1A 6
Newton Purcell. Oxon —1C 5
Newton Stacey. Hants —1A 32
Newton Valence. Hants —2D 33
Newtown. Hants —1B 42
(nr. Bishop's Waltham)
Newtown. Hants —2A 22
(nr. Newbury)
Newtown. Hants —2A 42
(nr. Warsash)
Newtown. Hants —1C 43
(nr. Wickham)
Newtown. IOW —3A 42
New Town. Lutn —2C 7
New Yatt. Oxon —3A 4
Newyears Green. G Lon —3C 17
Nine Ashes. Essx —1D 19
Ninfield. E Sus —1B 48
Ningwood. IOW —3A 42
Noak Hill. G Lon —2D 19
Noke. Oxon —3B 4
Nonington. Kent —3C 31
Norleywood. Hants —3A 42
Normandy. Surr —3B 24
Norman's Bay. E Sus —2A 48
Northall. Buck —2B 6
Northam. Sotn —1A 42
North Ascot. Brac —2B 24
North Aston. Oxon —2A 4
Northaw. Herts —1A 18
North Baddesley. Hants —3A 32
North Benfleet. Essx —3B 20
North Bersted. W Sus —2B 44
North Boarhunt. Hants —1C 43
Northbourne. Kent —3D 31
Northbourne. Oxon —3B 14
Northbrook. Oxon —2A 4
North Chailey. E Sus —3B 36
Northchapel. W Sus —3B 34
Northchurch. Herts —1B 16
North Common. E Sus —3B 36
Northcourt. Oxon —2B 14
North Cray. G Lon —1C 27
North End. Essx —3A 10
(nr. Great Dunmow)
North End. Essx —1B 10
(nr. Great Yeldham)
North End. Hants —2A 22
Northend. Oxon —2D 15
North End. Port —2C 43
North End. W Sus —2D 45
North Fambridge. Essx —2C 21
Northfleet. Kent —1A 28
North Halling. Medw —2B 28
North Hayling. Hants —2D 43
North Heath. W Sus —3C 35
North Hinksey. Oxon —1A 14
North Holmwood. Surr —1D 35
Northiam. E Sus —3C 39
Northington. Hants —2B 32
North Lancing. W Sus —2D 45
North Lee. Buck —1A 16
North Leigh. Kent —1B 40
North Leigh. Oxon —3A 4
North Marden. W Sus —1A 44
North Marston. Buck —2D 5
Northmoor. Oxon —1A 14
North Moreton. Oxon —3B 14
North Mundham. W Sus —2A 44
North Newington. Oxon —1A 4
Northney. Hants —2D 43
North Oakley. Hants —3B 22
North Ockendon. G Lon —3D 19
Northolt. G Lon —3D 17
North Sheen. G Lon —1D 25
North Shoebury. Essx —3D 21
North Stifford. Thur —3A 20
North Stoke. Medw —1C 29
North Stoke. Oxon —3C 15
North Stoke. W Sus —1C 45
North Street. Hants —2C 33
North Street. Kent —3A 30
North Street. Medw —1C 29
North Street. W Ber —1C 23
North Waltham. Hants —1B 32
North Warnborough. Hants —3D 23
North Weald Bassett. Essx —1D 19
Northwood. G Lon —2C 17
Northwood. IOW —3A 42
Northwood. Kent —2D 31
Norton. Herts —1A 8
Norton. W Sus —2B 44
(nr. Arundel)
Norton. W Sus —3A 44
(nr. Selsey)
Norton Heath. Essx —1A 20
Norton Mandeville. Essx —1D 19
Norwood Hill. Surr —1A 36
Nounsley. Essx —3B 10
Nuffield. Oxon —3C 15
Nuneham Courtenay. Oxon —2B 14
Nursling. Hants —1A 42
Nursted. Hants —3D 33
Nutbourne. W Sus —2D 43
(nr. Chichester)
Nutbourne. W Sus —1C 45
(nr. Pulborough)
Nutfield. Surr —3B 26
Nuthampstead. Herts —1C 9
Nuthurst. W Sus —3D 35
Nutley. E Sus —3C 37
Nyetimber. W Sus —3A 44
Nyewood. W Sus —3A 34
Nyton. W Sus —2B 44

Oad Street. Kent —2C 29
Oakhanger. Hants —2D 33
Oakley. Buck —3C 5
Oakley. Hants —3B 22
Oakley Green. Wind —1B 24
Oakshott. Hants —3D 33
Oakwoodhill. Surr —2D 35
Oare. Kent —2A 30
Oare. W Ber —1B 22
Ockham. Surr —3C 25
Ockley. Surr —1D 35
Oddington. Oxon —3B 4
Odiham. Hants —3D 23
Odsey. Cambs —1A 8
Offham. E Sus —1C 47
Offham. Kent —3A 28
Offham. W Sus —2C 45
Offley Hoo. Herts —2D 7
Old Alresford. Hants —2B 32
Old Basing. Hants —3C 23
Old Bexley. G Lon —1C 27
Old Burghclere. Hants —3A 22
Old Coulsdon. G Lon —3B 26
Old Felixstowe. Suff —1D 13
Old Grimsbury. Oxon —1A 4
Old Heathfield. E Sus —3D 37
Old Knebworth. Herts —2A 8
Old Romney. Kent —3A 40
Old Stratford. Nptn —1D 5
Old Town. E Sus —3D 47
Old Warden. Beds —1D 7
Old Windsor. Wind —1B 24
Old Wives Lees. Kent —3A 30
Old Woking. Surr —3C 25
Old Woodstock. Oxon —3A 4
Oliver's Battery. Hants —3A 32
Olmstead Green. Cambs —1A 10
Onslow Village. Surr —1B 34
Ore. E Sus —1C 49
Oreham Common. W Sus —1A 46
Orlestone. Kent —2D 39
Orpington. G Lon —2C 27
Orsett. Thur —3A 20
Ospringe. Kent —2A 30
Ostend. Essx —2D 21
Osterley. G Lon —1D 25
Otford. Kent —3D 27
Otham. Kent —3B 28
Otterbourne. Hants —3A 32
Otterham Quay. Kent —2C 29
Ottershaw. Surr —2C 25
Otterwood. Hants —2A 42
Ottinge. Kent —1B 40
Outwood. Surr —1B 36
Over Kiddington. Oxon —2A 4
Oversland. Kent —3A 30
Overthorpe. Nptn —1A 4
Overton. Hants —1B 32
Over Worton. Oxon —2A 4
Oving. Buck —2D 5
Oving. W Sus —2B 44
Ovingdean. Brig —2B 46
Ovington. Essx —1B 10
Ovington. Hants —2B 32
Ower. Hants —2A 42
Owlswick. Buck —1D 15
Ownham. W Ber —1A 22
Owslebury. Hants —3B 32
Oxen End. Essx —2A 10
Oxford. Oxon —1B 14
Oxhey. Herts —2D 17
Oxley Green. Essx —3D 11
Oxley's Green. E Sus —3A 38
Oxshott. Surr —2D 25
Oxted. Surr —3B 26

Pachesham. Surr —3D 25
Padbury. Buck —1D 5
Paddington. G Lon —3A 18
Paddlesworth. Kent —2B 40
Paddock. Kent —3D 29
Paddock Wood. Kent —1A 38
Padworth. W Ber —2C 23
Pagham. W Sus —3A 44
Paglesham Churchend. Essx —2D 21
Paglesham Eastend. Essx —2D 21
Paine's Corner. E Sus —3A 38
Painter's Forstal. Kent —3D 29
Palehouse Common. E Sus —1C 47

Paley Street. *Wind* —1A **24**
Palmarsh. *Kent* —2B **40**
Pamber End. *Hants* —3C **23**
Pamber Green. *Hants* —3C **23**
Pamber Heath. *Hants* —2C **23**
Panfield. *Essx* —2B **10**
Pangbourne. *W Ber* —1C **23**
Paramour Street. *Kent* —2C **31**
Parbrook. *W Sus* —3C **35**
Pardown. *Hants* —1B **32**
Park Corner. *E Sus* —2D **37**
Park Corner. *Oxon* —3C **15**
Parkeston. *Essx* —1C **13**
Park Gate. *Hants* —2B **42**
Parkgate. *Surr* —1A **36**
Parkhurst. *IOW* —3A **42**
Park Street. *Herts* —1D **17**
Park Street. *W Sus* —2D **35**
Park Town. *Oxon* —1B **14**
Parmoor. *Buck* —3D **15**
Parsonage Green. *Essx* —3B **10**
Partridge Green. *W Sus* —1D **45**
Passenham. *Nptn* —1D **5**
Passfield. *Hants* —2A **34**
Passingford Bridge. *Essx* —2D **19**
Patcham. *Brig* —2B **46**
Patchetts Green. *Herts* —2D **17**
Patching. *W Sus* —2C **45**
Patmore Heath. *Herts* —2C **9**
Patrixbourne. *Kent* —3B **30**
Pattiswick. *Essx* —2C **11**
Peacehaven. *E Sus* —2C **47**
Peasemore. *W Ber* —1A **22**
Pease Pottage. *W Sus* —2A **36**
Peaslake. *Surr* —1C **35**
Peasmarsh. *E Sus* —3C **39**
Peasmarsh. *Surr* —1B **34**
Pebmarsh. *Essx* —1C **11**
Peckham Bush. *Kent* —3A **28**
Pedlinge. *Kent* —2B **40**
Peel Common. *Hants* —2B **42**
Peening Quarter. *Kent* —3C **39**
Pegsdon. *Beds* —1D **7**
Peldon. *Essx* —3D **11**
Pembury. *Kent* —1A **38**
Penge. *G Lon* —1B **26**
Penhurst. *E Sus* —1A **48**
Penn. *Buck* —2B **16**
Penn Street. *Buck* —2B **16**
Penshurst. *Kent* —1D **37**
Peper Harow. *Surr* —1B **34**
Perry Green. *Essx* —2C **11**
Perry Green. *Herts* —3C **9**
Perry Street. *Kent* —1A **28**
Perrywood. *Kent* —3A **30**
Petersfield. *Hants* —3D **33**
Peter's Green. *Herts* —3D **7**
Petham. *Kent* —3B **30**
Pett. *E Sus* —1C **49**
Petteridge. *Kent* —1A **38**
Petts Wood. *G Lon* —2C **27**
Petworth. *W Sus* —3B **34**
Pevensey. *E Sus* —2A **48**
Pevensey Bay. *E Sus* —2A **48**
Pheasant's Hill. *Buck* —3D **15**
Phoenix Green. *Hants* —3D **23**
Piccotts End. *Herts* —1C **17**
Picket Piece. *Hants* —1A **32**
Piddinghoe. *E Sus* —2C **47**
Piddington. *Buck* —2A **16**
Piddington. *Oxon* —3C **5**
Pilgrims Hatch. *Essx* —2D **19**
Piltdown. *E Sus* —3C **37**
Pinkneys Green. *Wind* —3A **16**
Pin Mill. *Suff* —1C **13**
Pinner. *G Lon* —3D **17**
Pirbright. *Surr* —3B **24**
Pirton. *Herts* —1D **7**
Pishill. *Oxon* —3D **15**
Pitchcott. *Buck* —2D **5**
Pitch Green. *Buck* —1D **15**
Pitch Place. *Surr* —3B **24**
Pitsea. *Essx* —3B **20**
Pitstone. *Buck* —3B **6**
Pitstone Green. *Buck* —3B **6**
Pitt. *Hants* —3A **32**
Pittswood. *Kent* —1A **38**
Plaistow. *W Sus* —2C **35**
Plastow Green. *Hants* —2B **22**
Platt. *Kent* —3A **28**
Platt's Heath. *Kent* —3C **29**
Platt, The. *E Sus* —2D **37**
Plaxtol. *Kent* —3A **28**
Playden. *E Sus* —3D **39**
Play Hatch. *Oxon* —1D **23**
Pledgdon Green. *Essx* —2D **9**
Pleshey. *Essx* —3A **10**
Pluckley. *Kent* —1D **39**
Plummers Plain. *W Sus* —3A **36**
Plumpton. *E Sus* —1B **46**
Plumpton Green. *E Sus* —1B **46**
Plumstead. *G Lon* —1C **27**
Poffley End. *Oxon* —3A **4**
Point Clear. *Essx* —3A **12**
Polegate. *E Sus* —2D **47**
Poling. *W Sus* —2C **45**
Poling Corner. *W Sus* —2C **45**
Pollicott. *Buck* —3D **5**
Polstead. *Suff* —1D **11**
Polstead Heath. *Suff* —1D **11**
Ponders End. *G Lon* —2B **18**
Pond Street. *Essx* —1C **9**
Pondtail. *Hants* —3A **24**
Ponts Green. *E Sus* —1A **48**
Pooksgreen. *Hants* —1A **42**
Pool Street. *Essx* —1B **10**
Pootings. *Kent* —1C **37**
Popeswood. *Brac* —2A **24**
Popham. *Hants* —1B **32**
Poplar. *G Lon* —3B **18**
Popley. *Hants* —3C **23**
Porchfield. *IOW* —3A **42**
Portchester. *Hants* —2C **43**
Portsea. *Port* —2C **43**
Portslade-by-Sea. *Brig* —2A **46**
Portsmouth. *Port* —3C **43**
Portswood. *Sotn* —1A **42**
Postcombe. *Oxon* —2D **15**
Postling. *Kent* —2B **40**
Potsgrove. *Beds* —2B **6**
Potten End. *Herts* —1C **17**
Potters Bar. *Herts* —1A **18**
Potters Crouch. *Herts* —1D **17**
Potterspury. *Nptn* —1D **5**
Potter Street. *Essx* —1C **19**
Poundfield. *E Sus* —2D **37**
Poundgate. *E Sus* —3C **37**
Pound Green. *E Sus* —3D **37**
Pound Hill. *W Sus* —2A **36**
Poundon. *Buck* —2C **5**
Pound Street. *Hants* —2A **22**
Pounsley. *E Sus* —3D **37**
Poyle. *Buck* —1C **25**
Poynings. *W Sus* —1A **46**
Pratt's Bottom. *G Lon* —2C **27**
Preston. *Brig* —2B **46**
Preston. *Herts* —2D **7**
Preston. *Kent* —2C **31**
(nr. Canterbury)
Preston. *Kent* —2A **30**
(nr. Faversham)
Preston Bissett. *Buck* —2C **5**
Preston Candover. *Hants* —1C **33**
Prestwood. *Buck* —1A **16**
Priestwood. *Brac* —2A **24**
Priestwood. *Kent* —2A **28**
Princes Risborough. *Buck* —1A **16**
Prinsted. *W Sus* —2D **43**
Prittlewell. *S'end* —3C **21**
Privett. *Hants* —3C **33**
Puckeridge. *Herts* —2B **8**
Pulborough. *W Sus* —1C **45**
Pulloxhill. *Beds* —1C **7**
Punnett's Town. *E Sus* —3A **38**
Purbrook. *Hants* —2C **43**
Purfleet. *Thur* —1D **27**
Purleigh. *Essx* —1C **21**
Purley. *G Lon* —2B **26**
Purley. *W Ber* —1C **23**
Pusey. *Oxon* —2A **14**
Putney. *G Lon* —1A **26**
Puttenham. *Herts* —3A **6**
Puttenham. *Surr* —1B **34**
Puttock End. *Essx* —1C **11**
Puttock's End. *Essx* —3D **9**
Pyecombe. *W Sus* —1A **46**
Pye Corner. *Herts* —3C **9**
Pyrford. *Surr* —3C **25**
Pyrton. *Oxon* —2C **15**

Quainton. *Buck* —2D **5**
Quarrendon. *Buck* —3A **6**
Queenborough. *Kent* —1D **29**
Queen Street. *Kent* —1A **38**
Quendon. *Essx* —1D **9**
Quick's Green. *W Ber* —1B **22**
Quidhampton. *Hants* —3B **22**

Rableyheath. *Herts* —3A **8**
Rackham. *W Sus* —1C **45**
Radlett. *Herts* —2D **17**
Radley. *Oxon* —2B **14**
Radnage. *Buck* —2D **15**
Radstone. *Nptn* —1B **4**
Radwell. *Herts* —1A **8**
Radwinter. *Essx* —1A **10**
Rainham. *G Lon* —3D **19**
Rainham. *Medw* —2C **29**
Rake. *W Sus* —3A **34**
Ram Lane. *Kent* —1D **39**
Ramsdean. *Hants* —3D **33**
Ramsdell. *Hants* —3B **22**
Ramsden. *Oxon* —3A **4**
Ramsden Bellhouse. *Essx* —2B **20**
Ramsden Heath. *Essx* —2B **20**
Ramsey. *Essx* —1C **13**
Ramsey Island. *Essx* —1D **21**
Ramsgate. *Kent* —2D **31**
Ramsnest Common. *Surr* —2B **34**
Rank's Green. *Essx* —3B **10**
Ranmore Common. *Surr* —3D **25**
Ratton Village. *E Sus* —2D **47**
Rawreth. *Essx* —2B **20**
Raydon. *Suff* —1A **12**
Rayleigh. *Essx* —2C **21**
Rayne. *Essx* —2B **10**
Rayners Lane. *G Lon* —3D **17**
Reading. *Read* —1D **23**
Reading Street. *Kent* —2D **39**
Reculver. *Kent* —2C **31**
Redbourn. *Herts* —3D **7**
Redford. *W Sus* —3A **34**
Redhill. *Herts* —1A **8**
Redhill. *Surr* —3A **26**
Reed. *Herts* —1B **8**
Reed End. *Herts* —1B **8**
Reigate. *Surr* —3A **26**
Remenham. *Wok* —3D **15**
Remenham Hill. *Wok* —3D **15**
Rettendon. *Essx* —2B **20**
Rew Street. *IOW* —3A **42**
Rhodes Minnis. *Kent* —1B **40**
Richborough Port. *Kent* —2D **31**
Richings Park. *Buck* —1C **25**
Richmond. *G Lon* —1D **25**
Rickling. *Essx* —1C **9**
Rickling Green. *Essx* —2D **9**
Rickmansworth. *Herts* —2C **17**
Ridge. *Herts* —1A **18**
Ridgewell. *Essx* —1B **10**
Ridgewood. *E Sus* —3C **37**
Ridgmont. *Beds* —1B **6**
Ridley. *Kent* —2A **28**
Ringlestone. *Kent* —3C **29**
Ringmer. *E Sus* —1C **47**
Ringshall. *Buck* —3B **6**
Ringwould. *Kent* —1D **41**
Ripe. *E Sus* —1D **47**
Ripley. *Surr* —3C **25**
Riplington. *Hants* —3C **33**
Ripple. *Kent* —1D **41**
Riseden. *E Sus* —2A **38**
Riseden. *Kent* —2B **38**
Riseley. *Wok* —2D **23**
Rivenhall. *Essx* —3C **11**
Rivenhall End. *Essx* —3C **11**
River. *Kent* —1C **41**
River. *W Sus* —3B **34**
Riverhead. *Kent* —3D **27**
Robertsbridge. *E Sus* —3B **38**
Robinhood End. *Essx* —1B **10**
Rochester. *Medw* —2B **28**
Rochford. *Essx* —2C **21**
Rock. *W Sus* —1D **45**
Rockwell End. *Buck* —3D **15**
Rodmell. *E Sus* —2C **47**
Rodmersham. *Kent* —2D **29**
Rodmersham Green. *Kent* —2D **29**
Roe Green. *Herts* —1B **8**
Roehampton. *G Lon* —1A **26**
Roffey. *W Sus* —2D **35**
Rogate. *W Sus* —3A **34**
Roke. *Oxon* —2C **15**
Rokemarsh. *Oxon* —2C **15**
Rolvenden. *Kent* —2C **39**
Rolvenden Layne. *Kent* —2C **39**
Romford. *G Lon* —3D **19**
Romsey. *Hants* —3A **32**
Rookwood. *W Sus* —3D **43**
Ropley. *Hants* —2C **33**
Ropley Dean. *Hants* —2C **33**
Rose Green. *Essx* —2C **11**
Rose Hill. *E Sus* —1C **47**
Roser's Cross. *E Sus* —3D **37**
Rotherfield. *E Sus* —3D **37**
Rotherfield Greys. *Oxon* —3D **15**
Rotherfield Peppard. *Oxon* —3D **15**
Rotherwick. *Hants* —3D **23**
Rotten Row. *W Ber* —1B **22**
Rottingdean. *Brig* —2B **46**
Rough Common. *Kent* —3B **30**
Roundbush Green. *Essx* —3D **9**
Roundhurst Common. *W Sus* —2B **34**
Roundstreet Common. *W Sus* —3C **35**
Rousham. *Oxon* —2A **4**
Rout's Green. *Buck* —2D **15**
Row Ash. *Hants* —1B **42**
Row Green. *Essx* —2B **10**
Row Heath. *Essx* —3B **12**
Rowhedge. *Essx* —2A **12**
Rowhook. *W Sus* —2D **35**
Rowland's Castle. *Hants* —1D **43**
Rowledge. *Surr* —1A **34**
Rowly. *Surr* —1C **35**
Rowner. *Hants* —2B **42**
Rownhams. *Hants* —1A **42**
Rowsham. *Buck* —3A **6**
Rowstock. *Oxon* —3A **14**
Row Town. *Surr* —2C **25**
Roxwell. *Essx* —1A **20**
Royal Tunbridge Wells. *Kent* —2D **37**
Roydon. *Essx* —3C **9**
Roydon Hamlet. *Essx* —1C **19**
Royston. *Herts* —1B **8**
Ruckinge. *Kent* —2A **40**
Rucklers Lane. *Herts* —1C **17**
Rudgwick. *W Sus* —2C **35**
Rudley Green. *Essx* —1C **21**
Ruislip. *G Lon* —3C **17**
Ruislip Common. *G Lon* —3C **17**
Runcton. *W Sus* —2A **44**
Runfold. *Surr* —1A **34**
Runwell. *Essx* —2B **20**
Ruscombe. *Wok* —1D **23**
Rushden. *Herts* —1B **8**
Rushenden. *Kent* —1D **29**
Rush Green. *Herts* —2A **8**
Rushlake Green. *E Sus* —1A **48**
Rushmoor. *Surr* —1A **34**
Rusper. *W Sus* —2A **36**
Russell's Water. *Oxon* —3D **15**
Russ Hill. *Surr* —1A **36**
Rusthall. *Kent* —2D **37**
Rustington. *W Sus* —2C **45**
Ryarsh. *Kent* —3A **28**
Ryde. *IOW* —3B **42**
Rye. *E Sus* —3D **39**
Rye Foreign. *E Sus* —3D **39**
Rye Harbour. *E Sus* —1D **49**

Sacombe. *Herts* —3B **8**
Saddlescombe. *W Sus* —1A **46**
Saffron Walden. *Essx* —1D **9**
St Albans. *Herts* —1D **17**
St Cross. *Hants* —3A **32**
St Giles Hill. *Hants* —3A **32**
St Helens. *E Sus* —1C **49**
St Helens. *IOW* —3C **43**
Saint Hill. *W Sus* —2B **36**
St Ippollitts. *Herts* —2D **7**
St Lawrence. *Essx* —1D **21**
St Leonards. *Buck* —1B **16**
St Leonards. *E Sus* —2B **48**
St Margaret's. *Herts* —3C **7**
(nr. Hemel Hempstead)
St Margarets. *Herts* —3B **8**
(nr. Hoddesdon)
St Margaret's at Cliffe. *Kent* —1D **41**
St Mary Bourne. *Hants* —3A **22**
St Mary Cray. *G Lon* —2C **27**
St Mary Hoo. *Medw* —1C **29**
St Mary in the Marsh. *Kent* —3A **40**
St Mary's Bay. *Kent* —3A **40**
St Michaels. *Kent* —2C **39**
St Nicholas at Wade. *Kent* —2C **31**
St Osyth. *Essx* —3B **12**
St Osyth Heath. *Essx* —3B **12**
St Paul's Cray. *G Lon* —2C **27**
St Paul's Walden. *Herts* —2D **7**
St Peter's. *Kent* —2D **31**
Salcott. *Essx* —3D **11**
Salehurst. *E Sus* —3B **38**
Salford. *Beds* —1B **6**
Salfords. *Surr* —1A **36**
Saltdean. *Brig* —2B **46**
Saltwood. *Kent* —2B **40**
Sanderstead. *G Lon* —2B **26**
Sandford-on-Thames. *Oxon* —1B **14**
Sandford St Martin. *Oxon* —2A **4**
Sandgate. *Kent* —2B **40**
Sandhills. *Surr* —2B **34**
Sandhurst. *Brac* —2A **24**
Sandhurst. *Kent* —3B **38**
Sandhurst Cross. *Kent* —3B **38**
Sandleigh. *Oxon* —1A **14**
Sandling. *Kent* —3B **28**
Sandon. *Essx* —1B **20**
Sandon. *Herts* —1B **8**
Sandridge. *Herts* —3D **7**
Sands, The. *Surr* —1A **34**
Sandway. *Kent* —3C **29**
Sandwich. *Kent* —3D **31**
Sarisbury. *Hants* —2B **42**
Sarratt. *Herts* —2C **17**
Sarre. *Kent* —2C **31**
Satwell. *Oxon* —3D **15**
Saunderton. *Buck* —1D **15**
Saunderton Lee. *Buck* —2A **16**
Sawbridgeworth. *Herts* —3C **9**
Sayers Common. *W Sus* —1A **46**
Scayne's Hill. *W Sus* —3B **36**
School Green. *Essx* —1B **10**
Seabrook. *Kent* —2B **40**
Seaford. *E Sus* —3C **47**
Seal. *Kent* —3D **27**

Seale. *Surr* —1A **34**
Seasalter. *Kent* —2A **30**
Seaview. *IOW* —3C **43**
Seawick. *Essx* —3B **12**
Sedlescombe. *E Sus* —1B **48**
Seer Green. *Buck* —2B **16**
Selborne. *Hants* —2D **33**
Selham. *W Sus* —3B **34**
Sellindge. *Kent* —2A **40**
Selling. *Kent* —3A **30**
Selmeston. *E Sus* —2D **47**
Selsdon. *G Lon* —2B **26**
Selsey. *W Sus* —3A **44**
Selsfield Common. *W Sus*
—2B **36**
Selsted. *Kent* —1C **41**
Send. *Surr* —3C **25**
Send Marsh. *Surr* —3C **25**
Sennicotts. *W Sus* —2A **44**
Sevenoaks. *Kent* —3D **27**
Sevenoaks Weald. *Kent*
—3D **27**
Sevington. *Kent* —1A **40**
Sewards End. *Essx* —1D **9**
Sewardstone. *Essx* —2B **18**
Sewell. *Beds* —2B **6**
Shabbington. *Buck* —1C **15**
Shackleford. *Surr* —1B **34**
Shadoxhurst. *Kent* —2D **39**
Shalden. *Hants* —1C **33**
Shalfleet. *IOW* —3A **42**
Shalford. *Essx* —2B **10**
Shalford. *Surr* —1C **35**
Shalford Green. *Essx* —2B **10**
Shalmsford Street. *Kent*
—3A **30**
Shalstone. *Buck* —1C **5**
Shamley Green. *Surr* —1C **35**
Sharnal Street. *Medw* —1B **28**
Sharpenhoe. *Beds* —1C **7**
Sharpthorne. *W Sus* —2B **36**
Shaw. *W Ber* —2A **22**
Shawford. *Hants* —3A **32**
Shedfield. *Hants* —1B **42**
Sheering. *Essx* —3D **9**
Sheerness. *Kent* —1D **29**
Sheerwater. *Surr* —2C **25**
Sheet. *Hants* —3D **33**
Sheffield Bottom. *W Ber*
—2C **23**
Sheffield Green. *E Sus*
—3C **37**
Shefford. *Beds* —1D **7**
Shefford Woodlands. *W Ber*
—1A **22**
Sheldwich. *Kent* —3A **30**
Sheldwich Lees. *Kent* —3A **30**
Shelley. *Suff* —1A **12**
Shellow Bowells. *Essx*
—1A **20**
Shenfield. *Essx* —2A **20**
Shenington. *Oxon* —1A **4**
Shenley. *Herts* —1D **17**
Shenley Brook End. *Mil*
—1A **6**
Shenleybury. *Herts* —1D **17**
Shenley Church End. *Mil*
—1A **6**
Shephall. *Herts* —2A **8**
Shepherd's Bush. *G Lon*
—3A **18**
Shepherd's Green. *Oxon*
—3D **15**
Shepherdswell. *Kent* —1C **41**
Shepperton. *Surr* —2C **25**
Shepway. *Kent* —3B **28**
Sherborne St John. *Hants*
—3C **23**
Shere. *Surr* —1C **35**
Sherfield on Loddon. *Hants*
—3C **23**
Shermanbury. *W Sus* —1A **46**
Shillingford. *Oxon* —2B **14**
Shillington. *Beds* —1D **7**
Shinfield. *Wok* —2D **23**
Shingle Street. *Suff* —1D **13**
Shipbourne. *Kent* —3D **27**
Shiplake. *Oxon* —1D **23**
Shipley. *W Sus* —3D **35**
Shipley Bridge. *Surr* —1B **36**
Shippon. *Oxon* —2A **14**

Shipton. *Buck* —2D **5**
Shipton Green. *W Sus*
—3A **44**
Shipton-on-Cherwell. *Oxon*
—3A **4**
Shirburn. *Oxon* —2C **15**
Shirkoak. *Kent* —2D **39**
Shirley. *Sotn* —1A **42**
Shirrell Heath. *Hants* —1B **42**
Shoeburyness. *S'end*
—3D **21**
Sholden. *Kent* —3D **31**
Sholing. *Sotn* —1A **42**
Shoreditch. *G Lon* —3B **18**
Shoreham. *Kent* —2D **27**
Shoreham-by-Sea. *W Sus*
—2A **46**
Shorne. *Kent* —1A **28**
Shorne Ridgeway. *Kent*
—1A **28**
Shortbridge. *E Sus* —3C **37**
Shortgate. *E Sus* —1C **47**
Shotgate. *Essx* —2B **20**
Shotley. *Suff* —1C **13**
Shotley Gate. *Suff* —1C **13**
Shottenden. *Kent* —3A **30**
Shottermill. *Surr* —2A **34**
Shotttford. *Oxon* —1A **4**
Shreding Green. *Buck*
—3C **17**
Shripney. *W Sus* —2B **44**
Shrub End. *Essx* —2D **11**
Shurlock Row. *Wind* —1A **24**
Shutford. *Oxon* —1A **4**
Sibertswold. *Kent* —1C **41**
Sibford Ferris. *Oxon* —1A **4**
Sibford Gower. *Oxon* —1A **4**
Sible Hedingham. *Essx*
—1B **10**
Sidcup. *G Lon* —1C **27**
Sidlesham. *W Sus* —3A **44**
Sidley. *E Sus* —2B **48**
Sidlowbridge. *Surr* —1A **36**
Silchester. *Hants* —2C **23**
Silsoe. *Beds* —1C **7**
Silver End. *Essx* —3C **11**
Sindlesham. *Wok* —2D **23**
Singleborough. *Buck* —1D **5**
Singleton. *Kent* —1D **39**
Singleton. *W Sus* —1A **44**
Singlewell. *Kent* —1A **28**
Sinkhurst Green. *Kent*
—1C **39**
Sipson. *G Lon* —1C **25**
Sissinghurst. *Kent* —2B **38**
Sittingbourne. *Kent* —2D **29**
Skirmett. *Buck* —2D **15**
Skittle Green. *Buck* —1D **15**
Skye Green. *Essx* —2C **11**
Slade End. *Oxon* —2B **14**
Slade Green. *G Lon* —1D **27**
Slade, The. *W Ber* —1B **22**
Slapton. *Buck* —2B **6**
Slaugham. *W Sus* —3A **36**
Sleaford. *Hants* —2A **34**
Slindon. *W Sus* —2B **44**
Slinfold. *W Sus* —2D **35**
Slip End. *Herts* —3C **7**
Slough. *Slo* —1B **24**
Slough Green. *W Sus* —3A **36**
Small Dole. *W Sus* —1A **46**
Smallfield. *Surr* —1B **36**
Small Hythe. *Kent* —2C **39**
Smannell. *Hants* —1A **32**
Smarden. *Kent* —1C **39**
Smarden Bell. *Kent* —1C **39**
Smart's Hill. *Kent* —1D **37**
Smeeth. *Kent* —2A **40**
Smith's Green. *Essx* —2D **9**
Smyth's Green. *Essx* —3D **11**
Snargate. *Kent* —3D **39**
Snave. *Kent* —3A **40**
Snodland. *Kent* —2A **28**
Soake. *Hants* —1C **43**
Soberton. *Hants* —1C **43**
Soberton Heath. *Hants*
—1C **43**
Soldridge. *Hants* —2C **33**
Solent Breezes. *Hants*
—2B **42**
Sole Street. *Kent* —2A **28**
(nr. Meopham)

Sole Street. *Kent* —1A **40**
(nr. Waltham)
Somerley. *W Sus* —3A **44**
Somerton. *Oxon* —2A **4**
Sompting. *W Sus* —2D **45**
Sonning. *Wok* —1D **23**
Sonning Common. *Oxon*
—3D **15**
Soulbury. *Buck* —2A **6**
Souldern. *Oxon* —1B **4**
Southall. *G Lon* —1D **25**
South Ambersham. *W Sus*
—3B **34**
Southampton. *Sotn* —1A **42**
Southampton Airport. *Hants*
—1A **42**
South Ascot. *Wind* —2B **24**
South Baddesley. *Hants*
—3A **42**
South Benfleet. *Essx* —3B **20**
South Bersted. *W Sus*
—2B **44**
Southborough. *Kent* —1D **37**
Southbourne. *W Sus* —2A **44**
Southchurch. *S'end* —3D **21**
South Common. *E Sus*
—1B **46**
Southcourt. *Buck* —3A **6**
South Darenth. *Kent* —2D **27**
Southease. *E Sus* —2C **47**
South End. *W Ber* —1B **22**
Southend (London) Airport.
Essx —3C **21**
Southend-on-Sea. *S'end*
—3C **21**
Southernden. *Kent* —1C **39**
Southey Green. *Essx* —1B **10**
South Fambridge. *Essx*
—2C **21**
South Fawley. *W Ber* —3A **14**
Southfleet. *Kent* —1A **28**
Southgate. *G Lon* —2B **18**
South Godstone. *Surr*
—1B **36**
South Green. *Essx* —2A **20**
(nr. Billericay)
South Green. *Essx* —3A **12**
(nr. Colchester)
South Green. *Kent* —2C **29**
South Hanningfield. *Essx*
—2B **20**
South Harting. *W Sus*
—1D **43**
South Hayling. *Hants*
—3D **43**
South Heath. *Buck* —1B **16**
South Heath. *Essx* —3B **12**
South Heighton. *E Sus*
—2C **47**
South Hinksey. *Oxon* —1B **14**
South Holmwood. *Surr*
—1D **35**
South Hornchurch. *G Lon*
—3D **19**
Southill. *Beds* —1D **7**
Southington. *Hants* —1B **32**
South Lancing. *W Sus*
—2D **45**
South Leigh. *Oxon* —1A **14**
South Malling. *E Sus* —1C **47**
South Mimms. *Herts* —1A **18**
Southminster. *Essx* —2D **21**
South Moreton. *Oxon* —3B **14**
South Mundham. *W Sus*
—2A **44**
South Newington. *Oxon*
—1A **4**
South Norwood. *G Lon*
—2B **26**
South Nutfield. *Surr* —1B **36**
South Ockendon. *Thur*
—3D **19**
South Oxhey. *Herts* —2D **17**
Southrope. *Hants* —1C **33**
Southsea. *Port* —3C **43**
South Stifford. *Thur* —1D **27**
South Stoke. *Oxon* —3B **14**
South Stoke. *W Sus* —1B **45**
South Street. *E Sus* —1B **46**
South Street. *Kent* —3A **30**
(nr. Faversham)

South Street. *Kent* —2B **30**
(nr. Whitstable)
South Town. *Hants* —2C **33**
South Warnborough. *Hants*
—1D **33**
Southwater. *W Sus* —3D **35**
Southwater Street. *W Sus*
—3D **35**
South Weald. *Essx* —2D **19**
South Weston. *Oxon* —2D **15**
Southwick. *Hants* —2C **43**
Southwick. *W Sus* —2A **46**
South Wonston. *Hants*
—2A **32**
South Woodham Ferrers.
Essx —2C **21**
Sparrow's Green. *E Sus*
—2A **38**
Sparsholt. *Hants* —2A **32**
Sparsholt. *Oxon* —3A **14**
Spear Hill. *W Sus* —1D **45**
Speen. *Buck* —2A **16**
Speen. *W Ber* —2A **22**
Speldhurst. *Kent* —1D **37**
Spellbrook. *Herts* —3C **9**
Spencers Wood. *Wok* —2D **23**
Spithurst. *E Sus* —1C **47**
Spreakley. *Surr* —1A **34**
Spring Vale. *IOW* —3C **43**
Stadhampton. *Oxon* —2C **15**
Stagden Cross. *Essx* —3A **10**
Staines. *Surr* —1C **25**
Stakes. *Hants* —2C **43**
Stalisfield Green. *Kent*
—3D **29**
Stambourne. *Essx* —1B **10**
Stanborough. *Herts* —3A **8**
Stanbridge. *Beds* —2B **6**
Standen. *Kent* —1C **39**
Standen Street. *Kent* —2C **39**
Standford. *Hants* —2A **34**
Standlake. *Oxon* —1A **14**
Standon. *Hants* —3A **32**
Standon. *Herts* —2B **8**
Standon Green End. *Herts*
—3B **8**
Stanford. *Beds* —1D **7**
Stanford. *Kent* —2B **40**
Stanford Dingley. *W Ber*
—1B **22**
Stanford in the Vale. *Oxon*
—2A **14**
Stanford-le-Hope. *Thur*
—3A **20**
Stanford Rivers. *Essx* —1D **19**
Stanmer. *Brig* —2B **46**
Stanmore. *G Lon* —2D **17**
Stanmore. *Hants* —3A **32**
Stanmore. *W Ber* —1A **22**
Stanstead Abbots. *Herts*
—3B **8**
Stansted. *Kent* —2A **28**
Stansted (London) Airport.
Essx —2D **9**
Stansted Mountfitchet. *Essx*
—2D **9**
Stanton Harcourt. *Oxon*
—1A **14**
Stanton St John. *Oxon*
—1B **14**
Stanway. *Essx* —2D **11**
Stanwell. *Surr* —1C **25**
Stanwell Moor. *Surr* —1C **25**
Staple. *Kent* —3C **31**
Staplecross. *E Sus* —3B **38**
Staplefield. *W Sus* —3A **36**
Stapleford. *Herts* —3B **8**
Stapleford Abbotts. *Essx*
—2D **19**
Stapleford Tawney. *Essx*
—2D **19**
Staplehurst. *Kent* —1B **38**
Staplers. *IOW* —3B **42**
Starling's Green. *Essx* —1C **9**
Start Hill. *Essx* —2D **9**
Stebbing. *Essx* —2A **10**
Stebbing Green. *Essx* —2A **10**
Stedham. *W Sus* —3A **34**
Steel Cross. *E Sus* —2D **37**
Steep. *Hants* —3D **33**
Steeple. *Essx* —1D **21**

Steeple Aston. *Oxon* —2A **4**
Steeple Barton. *Oxon* —2A **4**
Steeple Bumpstead. *Essx*
—1A **10**
Steeple Claydon. *Buck* —2C **5**
Steeple Morden. *Cambs*
—1A **8**
Stelling Minnis. *Kent* —1B **40**
Stepney. *G Lon* —3B **18**
Steppingley. *Beds* —1C **7**
Stevenage. *Herts* —2A **8**
Steventon. *Hants* —1B **32**
Steventon. *Oxon* —2A **14**
Stevington End. *Cambs*
—1D **9**
Stewartby. *Beds* —1C **7**
Stewkley. *Buck* —2A **6**
Stewkley Dean. *Buck* —2A **6**
Steyning. *W Sus* —1D **45**
Stickling Green. *Essx* —1C **9**
Stisted. *Essx* —2B **10**
Stock. *Essx* —2A **20**
Stockbridge. *Hants* —2A **32**
Stockbury. *Kent* —2C **29**
Stockcross. *W Ber* —2A **22**
Stocker's Head. *Kent* —3D **29**
Stocking Green. *Essx* —1D **9**
Stocking Pelham. *Herts*
—2C **9**
Stocks, The. *Kent* —3D **39**
Stockstreet. *Essx* —2C **11**
Stodmarsh. *Kent* —2C **31**
Stoke. *Hants* —3A **22**
(nr. Andover)
Stoke. *Hants* —2D **43**
(nr. South Hayling)
Stoke. *Medw* —1C **29**
Stoke-by-Nayland. *Suff*
—1D **11**
Stoke Charity. *Hants* —2A **32**
Stoke D'Abernon. *Surr*
—3D **25**
Stoke Hammond. *Buck*
—2A **6**
Stoke Lyne. *Oxon* —2A **4**
Stoke Mandeville. *Buck*
—3A **6**
Stokenchurch. *Buck* —2D **15**
Stoke Newington. *G Lon*
—3B **18**
Stoke Poges. *Buck* —3B **16**
Stoke Row. *Oxon* —3C **15**
Stoke Talmage. *Oxon* —2C **15**
Stondon Massey. *Essx*
—1D **19**
Stone. *Buck* —3D **5**
Stone. *Kent* —1D **27**
Stonebridge. *Surr* —1D **35**
Stone Cross. *E Sus* —2A **48**
Stone Cross. *Kent* —2D **37**
Stonegate. *E Sus* —3A **38**
Stone Hill. *Kent* —2A **40**
Stone in Oxney. *Kent* —3D **39**
Stoner Hill. *Hants* —3D **33**
Stonesfield. *Oxon* —3A **4**
Stones Green. *Essx* —2B **12**
Stone Street. *Kent* —3D **27**
Stone Street. *Suff* —1D **11**
Stoneyhills. *Essx* —2D **21**
Stonor. *Oxon* —3D **15**
Stony Stratford. *Mil* —1D **5**
Stopham. *W Sus* —1C **45**
Stopsley. *Lutn* —2D **7**
Storrington. *W Sus* —1C **45**
Stotfold. *Beds* —1A **8**
Stoughton. *Surr* —3B **24**
Stoughton. *W Sus* —1A **44**
Stow Maries. *Essx* —2C **21**
Stowting. *Kent* —1B **40**
Stratfield Mortimer. *W Ber*
—2C **23**
Stratfield Saye. *Hants* —2C **23**
Stratfield Turgis. *Hants*
—3C **23**
Stratford St Mary. *Suff*
—1A **12**
Stratton Audley. *Oxon* —2C **5**
Streat. *E Sus* —1B **46**
Streatham. *G Lon* —1A **26**
Streatley. *Beds* —2C **7**
Streatley. *W Ber* —3B **14**

Street End. *W Sus* —3A **44**
Strethall. *Essx* —1C **9**
Strood. *Kent* —2C **39**
Strood. *Medw* —2B **28**
Strood Green. *Surr* —1A **36**
Strood Green. *W Sus* —3C **35**
   (nr. Billingshurst)
Strood Green. *W Sus* —2D **35**
   (nr. Horsham)
Stroud. *Hants* —3D **33**
Stroud Green. *Essx* —2C **21**
Stubbington. *Hants* —2B **42**
Stubb's Cross. *Kent* —2D **39**
Studham. *Beds* —3C **7**
Stunts Green. *E Sus* —1A **48**
Sturmer. *Essx* —1A **10**
Sturry. *Kent* —2B **30**
Stutton. *Suff* —1B **12**
Sudbury. *Suff* —1C **11**
Sulham. *W Ber* —1C **23**
Sulhamstead. *W Ber* —2C **23**
Sullington. *W Sus* —1C **45**
Summersdale. *W Sus* —2A **44**
Sunbury. *Surr* —2D **25**
Sundon Park. *Lutn* —2C **7**
Sundridge. *Kent* —3C **27**
Sunningdale. *Wind* —2B **24**
Sunninghill. *Wind* —2B **24**
Sunningwell. *Oxon* —1A **14**
Sunnymead. *Oxon* —1B **14**
Sunnyside. *W Sus* —2B **36**
Surbiton. *G Lon* —2D **25**
Surrex. *Essx* —2C **11**
Sutton. *Buck* —1C **25**
Sutton. *E Sus* —3C **47**
Sutton. *G Lon* —2A **26**
Sutton. *Kent* —1D **41**
Sutton. *Oxon* —1A **14**
Sutton. *W Sus* —1B **44**
Sutton Abinger. *Surr* —1D **35**
Sutton at Hone. *Kent* —2D **27**
Sutton Courtenay. *Oxon*
   —2B **14**
Sutton Green. *Surr* —3C **25**
Sutton Scotney. *Hants*
   —2A **32**
Sutton Valence. *Kent* —1C **39**
Swalcliffe. *Oxon* —1A **4**
Swalecliffe. *Kent* —2B **30**
Swallowfield. *Wok* —2D **23**
Swampton. *Hants* —3A **22**
Swanbourne. *Buck* —2A **6**
Swanley. *Kent* —2D **27**
Swanmore. *Hants* —1B **42**
Swanscombe. *Kent* —1D **27**
Swan Street. *Essx* —2C **11**
Swanton Street. *Kent* —3C **29**
Swanwick. *Hants* —2B **42**
Swarraton. *Hants* —2B **32**
Swaythling. *Sotn* —1A **42**
Swerford. *Oxon* —1A **4**
Swiftsden. *E Sus* —3B **38**
Swinford. *Oxon* —1A **14**
Swingfield Minnis. *Kent*
   —1C **41**
Swingfield Street. *Kent*
   —1C **41**
Sydenham. *G Lon* —1B **26**
Sydenham. *Oxon* —1D **15**
Sydmonton. *Hants* —3A **22**
Syresham. *Nptn* —1C **5**

Tackley. *Oxon* —2A **4**
Tadley. *Hants* —2C **23**
Tadmarton. *Oxon* —1A **4**
Tadworth. *Surr* —3A **26**
Takeley. *Essx* —2D **9**
Takeley Street. *Essx* —2D **9**
Tandridge. *Surr* —3B **26**
Tangmere. *W Sus* —2B **44**
Tankerton. *Kent* —2B **30**
Taplow. *Buck* —3B **16**
Tarpots. *Essx* —3B **20**
Tarring Neville. *E Sus* —2C **47**
Taston. *Oxon* —2A **4**
Tatling End. *Buck* —3C **17**
Tatsfield. *Surr* —3C **27**
Tattingstone. *Suff* —1B **12**
Tattingstone White Horse.
   Suff —1B **12**

Taverners Green. *Essx* —3D **9**
Tebworth. *Beds* —2B **6**
Teddington. *G Lon* —1D **25**
Telham. *E Sus* —1B **48**
Telscombe. *E Sus* —2C **47**
Telscombe Cliffs. *E Sus*
   —2B **46**
Temple Ewell. *Kent* —1C **41**
Templeton. *W Ber* —2A **22**
Tendring. *Essx* —2B **12**
Tendring Green. *Essx* —2B **12**
Tenterden. *Kent* —2C **39**
Terling. *Essx* —3B **10**
Terrick. *Buck* —1A **16**
Teston. *Kent* —3B **28**
Testwood. *Hants* —1A **42**
Tetsworth. *Oxon* —1C **15**
Tewin. *Herts* —3A **8**
Teynham. *Kent* —2D **29**
Teynham Street. *Kent* —2D **29**
Thakeham. *W Sus* —1D **45**
Thame. *Oxon* —1D **15**
Thames Ditton. *Surr* —2D **25**
Thames Haven. *Thur* —3B **20**
Thamesmead. *G Lon* —1C **27**
Thamesport. *Medw* —1C **29**
Thanington. *Kent* —3B **30**
Thatcham. *W Ber* —2B **22**
Thaxted. *Essx* —1A **10**
Theale. *W Ber* —1C **23**
Thenford. *Nptn* —1B **4**
Therfield. *Herts* —1B **8**
Theydon Bois. *Essx* —2C **19**
Thong. *Kent* —1A **28**
Thorington Street. *Suff*
   —1A **12**
Thorley. *Herts* —3C **9**
Thorley Street. *Herts* —3C **9**
Thorley Street. *IOW* —3A **42**
Thornborough. *Buck* —1D **5**
Thorncombe Street. *Surr*
   —1B **34**
Thornhill. *Sotn* —1A **42**
Thornton. *Buck* —1D **5**
Thornton Heath. *G Lon*
   —2B **26**
Thornwood Common. *Essx*
   —1C **19**
Thorpe. *Surr* —2C **25**
Thorpe Bay. *S'end* —3D **21**
Thorpe Common. *Suff*
   —1C **13**
Thorpe Green. *Essx* —2B **12**
Thorpe-le-Soken. *Essx*
   —2B **12**
Thorrington. *Essx* —2A **12**
Three Bridges. *W Sus*
   —2A **36**
Three Chimneys. *Kent*
   —2C **39**
Three Cups Corner. *E Sus*
   —3A **38**
Three Leg Cross. *E Sus*
   —2A **38**
Three Mile Cross. *Wok*
   —2D **23**
Three Oaks. *E Sus* —1C **49**
Throcking. *Herts* —1B **8**
Throwley. *Kent* —3D **29**
Throwley Forstal. *Kent*
   —3D **29**
Thrupp. *Oxon* —3A **4**
Thundersley. *Essx* —3B **20**
Thurnham. *Kent* —3C **29**
Thursley. *Surr* —2B **34**
Ticehurst. *E Sus* —2A **38**
Tichborne. *Hants* —2B **32**
Tiddington. *Oxon* —1C **15**
Tidebrook. *E Sus* —3A **38**
Tidmarsh. *W Ber* —1C **23**
Tilbury. *Thur* —1A **28**
Tilehurst. *Read* —1C **23**
Tilford. *Surr* —1A **34**
Tilgate Forest Row. *W Sus*
   —3A **36**
Tillingham. *Essx* —1D **21**
Tillington. *W Sus* —3B **34**
Tilmanstone. *Kent* —3D **31**
Tilsworth. *Beds* —2B **6**
Timsbury. *Hants* —3A **32**
Tingewick. *Buck* —1C **5**

Tingrith. *Beds* —1C **7**
Tinsley Green. *W Sus*
   —2A **36**
Tiptree. *Essx* —3C **11**
Tiptree Heath. *Essx* —3C **11**
Tisman's Common. *W Sus*
   —2C **35**
Titchfield. *Hants* —2B **42**
Titsey. *Surr* —3C **27**
Toddington. *Beds* —2C **7**
Tokers Green. *Oxon* —1D **23**
Tollesbury. *Essx* —3D **11**
Tolleshunt D'Arcy. *Essx*
   —3D **11**
Tolleshunt Knights. *Essx*
   —3D **11**
Tolleshunt Major. *Essx*
   —3D **11**
Tolworth. *G Lon* —2D **25**
Tonbridge. *Kent* —1D **37**
Tongham. *Surr* —1A **34**
Tonwell. *Herts* —3B **8**
Toot Baldon. *Oxon* —1B **14**
Toot Hill. *Essx* —1D **19**
Toot Hill. *Hants* —1A **42**
Toppesfield. *Essx* —1B **10**
Tortington. *W Sus* —2C **45**
Tottenham. *G Lon* —2B **18**
Totteridge. *G Lon* —2A **18**
Totternhoe. *Beds* —2B **6**
Totton. *Hants* —1A **42**
Touchenend. *Wind* —1A **24**
Tower Hill. *W Sus* —3D **35**
Towersey. *Oxon* —1D **15**
Town Littleworth. *E Sus*
   —1C **47**
Town Row. *E Sus* —2D **37**
Towns End. *Hants* —3B **22**
Townsend. *Herts* —1D **17**
Toy's Hill. *Kent* —3C **27**
Trash Green. *W Ber* —2C **23**
Treyford. *W Sus* —1A **44**
Trimley Lower Street. *Suff*
   —1C **13**
Trimley St Martin. *Suff*
   —1C **13**
Trimley St Mary. *Suff* —1C **13**
Tring. *Herts* —3B **6**
Trottiscliffe. *Kent* —2A **28**
Trotton. *W Sus* —3A **34**
Trowley Bottom. *Herts* —3C **7**
Trumps Green. *Surr* —2B **24**
Tubney. *Oxon* —2A **14**
Tudeley. *Kent* —1A **38**
Tuesley. *Surr* —1B **34**
Tufton. *Hants* —1A **32**
Tumbler's Green. *Essx*
   —2C **11**
Tunstall. *Kent* —2C **29**
Tunworth. *Hants* —1C **33**
Turgis Green. *Hants* —3C **23**
Turkey Island. *Hants* —1B **42**
Turners Hill. *W Sus* —2B **36**
Turnford. *Herts* —1B **18**
Turville. *Buck* —2D **15**
Turville Heath. *Buck* —2D **15**
Turweston. *Buck* —1C **5**
Tutts Clump. *W Ber* —1B **22**
Twickenham. *G Lon* —1D **25**
Twineham. *W Sus* —3A **36**
Twinstead. *Essx* —1C **11**
Twinstead Green. *Essx*
   —1C **11**
Twyford. *Buck* —2C **5**
Twyford. *Hants* —3A **32**
Twyford. *Wok* —1D **23**
Tye. *Hants* —2D **43**
Tye Green. *Essx* —2D **9**
   (nr. Bishop's Stortford)
Tye Green. *Essx* —2B **10**
   (nr. Braintree)
Tye Green. *Essx* —1D **9**
   (nr. Saffron Walden)
Tyler Hill. *Kent* —2B **30**
Tylers Green. *Buck* —2A **16**
Tyler's Green. *Essx* —1D **19**

Uckfield. *E Sus* —3C **37**
Udimore. *E Sus* —1C **49**
Ufton Nervet. *W Ber* —2C **23**

Ugley. *Essx* —2D **9**
Ugley Green. *Essx* —2D **9**
Ulcombe. *Kent* —1C **39**
Ulting. *Essx* —1C **21**
Underriver. *Kent* —1D **27**
Union Street. *E Sus* —2B **38**
Upchurch. *Kent* —2C **29**
Upham. *Hants* —3B **32**
Uplees. *Kent* —2D **29**
Up Marden. *W Sus* —1D **43**
Upminster. *G Lon* —3D **19**
Up Nately. *Hants* —3C **23**
Upper Arncott. *Oxon* —3C **5**
Upper Astrop. *Nptn* —1B **4**
Upper Basildon. *W Ber*
   —1B **22**
Upper Beeding. *W Sus*
   —1D **45**
Upper Bucklebury. *W Ber*
   —2B **22**
Upper Bullington. *Hants*
   —1A **32**
Upper Clatford. *Hants*
   —1A **32**
Upper Cokeham. *W Sus*
   —2D **45**
Upper Dicker. *E Sus* —2D **47**
Upper Dovercourt. *Essx*
   —1C **13**
Upper Dunsley. *Herts* —3B **6**
Upper Enham. *Hants* —1A **32**
Upper Farringdon. *Hants*
   —2D **33**
Upper Froyle. *Hants* —1D **33**
Upper Gravenhurst. *Beds*
   —1D **7**
Upper Green. *Essx* —1C **9**
Upper Green. *W Ber* —2A **22**
Upper Hale. *Surr* —1A **34**
Upper Halliford. *Surr* —2C **25**
Upper Halling. *Medw* —2A **28**
Upper Hartfield. *E Sus*
   —2C **37**
Upper Heyford. *Oxon* —2A **4**
Upper Horsebridge. *E Sus*
   —1C **49**
Upper Layham. *Suff* —1A **12**
Upper North Dean. *Buck*
   —2A **16**
Upper Norwood. *W Sus*
   —1B **44**
Upper Stondon. *Beds* —1D **7**
Upper Street. *Suff* —1B **12**
Upper Sundon. *Beds* —2C **7**
Upperton. *W Sus* —3B **34**
Upper Tooting. *G Lon* —1A **26**
Upper Upnor. *Medw* —1B **28**
Upper Weald. *Mil* —1D **5**
Upper Wellingham. *E Sus*
   —1C **47**
Upper Wield. *Hants* —2C **33**
Upper Winchendon. *Buck*
   —3D **5**
Upper Wootton. *Hants*
   —3B **22**
Upshire. *Essx* —1C **19**
Up Somborne. *Hants* —2A **32**
Upstreet. *Kent* —2C **31**
Upton. *Buck* —3D **5**
Upton. *Hants* —3A **22**
   (nr. Andover)
Upton. *Hants* —1A **42**
   (nr. Southampton)
Upton. *IOW* —3B **42**
Upton. *Oxon* —3B **14**
Upton. *Slo* —1B **24**
Upton End. *Beds* —1D **7**
Upton Grey. *Hants* —1C **33**
Upwaltham. *W Sus* —1B **44**
Upwick Green. *Herts* —2C **9**
Uxbridge. *G Lon* —3C **17**

Valley End. *Surr* —2B **24**
Vange. *Essx* —3B **20**
Vernham Dean. *Hants*
   —3A **22**
Vernham Street. *Hants*
   —3A **22**
Vigo Village. *Kent* —2A **28**
Vinehall Street. *E Sus* —3B **38**

Vine's Cross. *E Sus* —1D **47**
Virginia Water. *Surr* —2B **24**

Waddesdon. *Buck* —3D **5**
Wadesmill. *Herts* —3B **8**
Wadhurst. *E Sus* —2A **38**
Wadwick. *Hants* —3A **22**
Wainscott. *Medw* —1B **28**
Wakes Colne. *Essx* —2C **11**
Walberton. *W Sus* —2B **44**
Walderslade. *Medw* —2B **28**
Walderton. *W Sus* —1D **43**
Waldron. *E Sus* —1D **47**
Walkern. *Herts* —2A **8**
Wallands Park. *E Sus* —1C **47**
Wallcrouch. *E Sus* —2A **38**
Wallend. *Medw* —1C **29**
Wallingford. *Oxon* —3C **15**
Wallington. *G Lon* —2A **26**
Wallington. *Hants* —2B **42**
Wallington. *Herts* —1A **8**
Walliswood. *Surr* —2D **35**
Walmer. *Kent* —3D **31**
Walsworth. *Herts* —1D **7**
Waltham. *Kent* —1B **40**
Waltham Abbey. *Essx* —1B **18**
Waltham Chase. *Hants*
   —1B **42**
Waltham Cross. *Herts*
   —1B **18**
Waltham St Lawrence. *Wind*
   —1A **24**
Waltham's Cross. *Essx*
   —1A **10**
Walthamstow. *G Lon* —3B **18**
Walton. *Mil* —1A **6**
Walton. *Suff* —1C **13**
Walton-on-Thames. *Surr*
   —2D **25**
Walton on the Hill. *Surr*
   —3A **26**
Walton-on-the-Naze. *Essx*
   —2C **13**
Wanborough. *Surr* —1B **34**
Wandsworth. *G Lon* —1A **26**
Wannock. *E Sus* —2D **47**
Wanshurst Green. *Kent*
   —1B **38**
Wanstead. *G Lon* —3C **19**
Wantage. *Oxon* —3A **14**
Warbleton. *E Sus* —1A **48**
Warblington. *Hants* —2D **43**
Warborough. *Oxon* —2B **14**
Warden. *Kent* —1A **30**
Wardhedges. *Beds* —1C **7**
Wardley. *W Sus* —3A **34**
Ware. *Herts* —3B **8**
Ware. *Kent* —2C **31**
Warehorne. *Kent* —2D **39**
Wareside. *Herts* —3B **8**
Warfield. *Brac* —1A **24**
Wargrave. *Wok* —1D **23**
Warkworth. *Nptn* —1A **4**
Warlingham. *Surr* —3B **26**
Warminghurst. *W Sus*
   —1D **45**
Warners End. *Herts* —1C **17**
Warnford. *Hants* —3C **33**
Warnham. *W Sus* —2D **35**
Warningcamp. *W Sus*
   —2C **45**
Warninglid. *W Sus* —3A **36**
Warren Corner. *Hants*
   (nr. Aldershot) —1A **34**
Warren Corner. *Hants*
   (nr. Petersfield) —3D **33**
Warren Row. *Wind* —3A **16**
Warren Street. *Kent* —3D **29**
Warsash. *Hants* —2A **42**
Wartling. *E Sus* —2A **48**
Warwick Wold. *Surr* —3B **26**
Washbrook. *Suff* —1B **12**
Wash Common. *W Ber*
   —2A **22**
Washington. *W Sus* —1D **45**
Wasp Green. *Surr* —1B **36**
Waterbeach. *W Sus* —2A **44**
Water End. *Beds* —1C **7**
Water End. *Herts* —1A **18**
   (nr. Hatfield)

Water End. *Herts* —3C **7**
(nr. Hemel Hempstead)
Waterford. *Herts* —3B **8**
Wateringbury. *Kent* —3A **28**
Waterlooville. *Hants* —2C **43**
Waterperry. *Oxon* —1C **15**
Watersfield. *W Sus* —1C **45**
Waterside. *Buck* —1B **16**
Waterstock. *Oxon* —1C **15**
Water Stratford. *Buck* —1C **5**
Watford. *Herts* —2C **17**
Watlington. *Oxon* —2C **15**
Watton at Stone. *Herts* —3A **8**
Wavendon. *Mil* —1B **6**
Waverley. *Surr* —1A **34**
Wealdstone. *G Lon* —2D **17**
Weedon. *Buck* —3A **6**
Weeke. *Hants* —2A **32**
Weeley. *Essx* —2B **12**
Weeley Heath. *Essx* —2B **12**
Welford. *W Ber* —1A **22**
Welham Green. *Herts* —1A **18**
Well. *Hants* —1D **33**
Well Hill. *Kent* —2C **27**
Wellhouse. *W Ber* —1B **22**
Welling. *G Lon* —1C **27**
Wellow. *IOW* —3A **42**
Wellpond Green. *Herts* —2C **9**
Welwyn. *Herts* —3A **8**
Welwyn Garden City. *Herts*
—3A **8**
Wembley. *G Lon* —3D **17**
Wendens Ambo. *Essx* —1D **9**
Wendlebury. *Oxon* —3B **4**
Wendover. *Buck* —1A **16**
Wennington. *G Lon* —3D **19**
Wepham. *W Sus* —2C **45**
West Ashling. *W Sus* —2A **44**
Westbere. *Kent* —2B **30**
West Bergholt. *Essx* —2D **11**
West Blatchington. *Brig*
—2A **46**
Westbourne. *W Sus* —2D **43**
West Brabourne. *Kent*
—1A **40**
Westbrook. *Kent* —1D **31**
West Burton. *W Sus* —1B **44**
Westbury. *Buck* —1C **5**
West Byfleet. *Surr* —2C **25**
West Challow. *Oxon* —3A **14**
West Chiltington. *W Sus*
—1C **45**
West Chiltington Common.
W Sus —1C **45**
West Clandon. *Surr* —3C **25**
West Cliffe. *Kent* —1D **41**
Westcliffe-on-Sea. *S'end*
—3C **21**
Westcot. *Oxon* —3A **14**
Westcott. *Buck* —3D **5**
Westcott. *Surr* —1D **35**
Westcott Barton. *Oxon* —2A **4**
Westdean. *E Sus* —3D **47**
West Dean. *W Sus* —1A **44**
West Drayton. *G Lon* —1C **25**
West End. *G Lon* —3A **18**
West End. *Hants* —1A **42**
West End. *Herts* —1A **18**
West End. *Kent* —2B **30**
West End. *Surr* —2B **24**
West End. *Wind* —1A **24**
West End Green. *Hants*
—2C **23**
Westenhanger. *Kent* —2B **40**
Westergate. *W Sus* —2B **44**
Westerham. *Kent* —3C **27**
Westerton. *W Sus* —2A **44**
West Farleigh. *Kent* —3B **28**
Westfield. *E Sus* —1C **49**
West Firle. *E Sus* —2C **47**
Westgate on Sea. *Kent*
—1D **31**
West Ginge. *Oxon* —3A **14**
West Green. *Hants* —3D **23**
West Grinstead. *W Sus*
—3D **35**
West Hagbourne. *Oxon*
—3B **14**
Westham. *E Sus* —2A **48**
West Ham. *G Lon* —3B **18**

Westhampnett. *W Sus*
—2A **44**
West Hanney. *Oxon* —2A **14**
West Hanningfield. *Essx*
—2B **20**
West Harting. *W Sus* —3D **33**
West Heath. *Hants* —3B **22**
(nr. Basingstoke)
West Heath. *Hants* —3A **24**
(nr. Farnborough)
West Hendred. *Oxon* —3A **14**
West Hill. *W Sus* —2B **36**
West Hoathly. *W Sus* —3A **8**
West Horndon. *Essx* —3A **20**
West Horsley. *Surr* —3C **25**
West Hougham. *Kent* —1C **41**
Westhumble. *Surr* —3D **25**
West Hyde. *Herts* —2C **17**
West Hythe. *Kent* —2B **40**
West Ilsley. *W Ber* —3A **14**
West Itchenor. *W Sus*
—2D **43**
West Kingsdown. *Kent*
—2D **27**
West Langdon. *Kent* —1D **41**
West Lavington. *W Sus*
—3A **34**
West Leith. *Herts* —3B **6**
Westlington. *Buck* —3D **5**
West Malling. *Kent* —3A **28**
West Marden. *W Sus* —1D **43**
Westmarsh. *Kent* —2C **31**
West Meon. *Hants* —3C **33**
West Mersea. *Essx* —3A **12**
Westmeston. *E Sus* —1B **46**
Westmill. *Herts* —2B **8**
(nr. Buntingford)
Westmill. *Herts* —1D **7**
(nr. Hitchin)
Westminster. *G Lon* —1A **26**
West Molesey. *Surr* —2D **25**
West Norwood. *G Lon*
—1B **26**
Weston. *Hants* —3D **33**
Weston. *Herts* —1A **8**
Weston. *W Ber* —1A **22**
Westoning. *Beds* —1C **7**
Weston-on-the-Green. *Oxon*
—3B **4**
Weston Patrick. *Hants*
—1C **33**
Weston Turville. *Buck* —3A **6**
West Peckham. *Kent* —3A **28**
West Stoke. *W Sus* —2A **44**
West Stourmouth. *Kent*
—2C **31**
West Stratton. *Hants* —1B **32**
West Street. *Kent* —3D **29**
West Thorney. *W Sus*
—2D **43**
West Thurrock. *Thur* —1D **27**
West Tilbury. *Thur* —1A **28**
West Tisted. *Hants* —3C **33**
West Town. *Hants* —3D **43**
Westwell. *Kent* —1D **39**
Westwell Leacon. *Kent*
—1D **39**
West Wickham. *G Lon*
—2B **26**
West Wittering. *W Sus*
—3D **43**
Westwood. *Kent* —2D **31**
West Woodhay. *W Ber*
—2A **22**
West Worldham. *Hants*
—2D **33**
West Worthing. *W Sus*
—2D **45**
West Wycombe. *Buck*
—2A **16**
Wethersfield. *Essx* —1B **10**
Wexham Street. *Buck* —3B **16**
Weybourne. *Surr* —1A **34**
Weybridge. *Surr* —2C **25**
Whaddon. *Buck* —1A **6**
Wharley End. *Beds* —1B **6**
Whatlington. *E Sus* —1B **48**
Wheathampstead. *Herts*
—3D **7**
Wheatley. *Hants* —1D **33**

Wheatley. *Oxon* —1B **14**
Wheelerstreet. *Surr* —1B **34**
Whelpley Hill. *Buck* —1B **16**
Wherstead. *Suff* —1B **12**
Wherwell. *Hants* —1A **32**
Whetsted. *Kent* —1A **38**
Whetstone. *G Lon* —2A **18**
Whippingham. *IOW* —3B **42**
Whipsnade. *Beds* —3C **7**
Whistley Green. *Wok* —1D **23**
Whitchurch. *Buck* —2A **6**
Whitchurch. *Hants* —1A **32**
Whitchurch. *Oxon* —1C **23**
Whitchurch Hill. *Oxon*
—1C **23**
Whiteash Green. *Essx*
—1B **10**
White Colne. *Essx* —2C **11**
Whitehall. *Hants* —3D **23**
Whitehall. *W Sus* —3D **35**
Whitehill. *Hants* —2D **33**
Whiteley. *Hants* —2B **42**
Whiteley Village. *Surr* —2C **25**
Whitemans Green. *W Sus*
—3B **36**
Whitenap. *Hants* —3A **32**
White Notley. *Essx* —3B **10**
White Roding. *Essx* —3D **9**
Whitesmith. *E Sus* —1D **47**
Whitestreet Green. *Suff*
—1D **11**
White Waltham. *Wind*
—1A **24**
Whitfield. *Kent* —1D **41**
Whitfield. *Nptn* —1C **5**
Whitstable. *Kent* —2B **30**
Whitway. *Hants* —3A **22**
Whitwell. *Herts* —2D **7**
Whyteleafe. *Surr* —3B **26**
Wichling. *Kent* —3D **29**
Wick. *W Sus* —2C **45**
Wicken. *Nptn* —1D **5**
Wicken Bonhunt. *Essx* —1C **9**
Wicker Street Green. *Suff*
—1D **11**
Wickford. *Essx* —2B **20**
Wickham. *Hants* —1B **42**
Wickham. *W Ber* —1A **22**
Wickham Bishops. *Essx*
—3C **11**
Wickhambreaux. *Kent*
—3C **31**
Wickham Heath. *W Ber*
—2A **22**
Wickham St Paul. *Essx*
—1C **11**
Wick Hill. *Wok* —2D **23**
Widdington. *Essx* —1D **9**
Widford. *Essx* —1A **20**
Widford. *Herts* —3C **9**
Widmer End. *Buck* —2A **16**
Wiggens Green. *Essx*
—1A **10**
Wigginton. *Herts* —3B **6**
Wigginton. *Oxon* —1A **4**
Wiggonholt. *W Sus* —1C **45**
Wigmore. *Medw* —2C **29**
Wildern. *Hants* —1A **42**
Wildhern. *Hants* —3A **22**
Willen. *Mil* —1A **6**
Willesborough. *Kent* —1A **40**
Willesborough Lees. *Kent*
—1A **40**
Willesden. *G Lon* —3A **18**
Willey Green. *Surr* —3B **24**
Willian. *Herts* —1A **8**
Willingale. *Essx* —1D **19**
Willingdon. *E Sus* —2D **47**
Willows Green. *Essx* —3B **10**
Wilmington. *E Sus* —2D **47**
Wilmington. *Kent* —1D **27**
Wilsley Green. *Kent* —2B **38**
Wilstead. *Beds* —1C **7**
Wilstone. *Herts* —3B **6**
Wimbish. *Essx* —1D **9**
Wimbish Green. *Essx* —1A **10**
Wimbledon. *G Lon* —1A **26**
Winchelsea. *E Sus* —1D **49**
Winchelsea Beach. *E Sus*
—1D **49**

Winchester. *Hants* —3A **32**
Winchet Hill. *Kent* —1B **38**
Winchfield. *Hants* —3D **23**
Winchmore Hill. *Buck*
—2B **16**
Winchmore Hill. *G Lon*
—2B **18**
Windlesham. *Surr* —2B **24**
Windmill Hill. *E Sus* —1A **48**
Windsor. *Wind* —1B **24**
Wineham. *W Sus* —3A **36**
Wing. *Buck* —2A **6**
Wingfield. *Beds* —2C **7**
Wingham. *Kent* —3C **31**
Wingmore. *Kent* —1B **40**
Wingrave. *Buck* —3A **6**
Winkfield. *Brac* —1B **24**
Winkfield Row. *Brac* —1A **24**
Winklebury. *Hants* —3C **23**
Winnersh. *Wok* —1D **23**
Winslade. *Hants* —1C **33**
Winslow. *Buck* —2D **5**
Winterbourne. *W Ber* —1A **22**
Winterbrook. *Oxon* —3C **15**
Winter Gardens. *Essx* —3B **20**
Winton. *E Sus* —2D **47**
Wisborough Green. *W Sus*
—3C **35**
Wisley. *Surr* —3C **25**
Wissenden. *Kent* —1D **39**
Wiston. *W Sus* —1D **45**
Witchampton. *Essx* —3C **11**
Witherenden Hill. *E Sus*
—3A **38**
Witheridge Hill. *Oxon* —3C **15**
Withermarsh Green. *Suff*
—1A **12**
Withyham. *E Sus* —2C **37**
Witley. *Surr* —1B **34**
Witney. *Oxon* —3A **4**
Wittersham. *Kent* —3D **39**
Wivelrod. *Hants* —2C **33**
Wivelsfield. *E Sus* —3B **36**
Wivelsfield Green. *E Sus*
—3B **36**
Wivenhoe. *Essx* —2A **12**
Wix. *Essx* —2B **12**
Wixoe. *Suff* —1B **10**
Woburn. *Beds* —1B **6**
Woburn Sands. *Mil* —1B **6**
Woking. *Surr* —2C **25**
Wokingham. *Wok* —2A **24**
Woldingham. *Surr* —3B **26**
Wolvercote. *Oxon* —1A **14**
Wolverton. *Hants* —3B **22**
Wolverton. *Mil* —1A **6**
Wolverton Common. *Hants*
—3B **22**
Womenswold. *Kent* —3C **31**
Wonersh. *Surr* —1C **35**
Wonston. *Hants* —2A **32**
Wooburn. *Buck* —3B **16**
Wooburn Green. *Buck*
—3B **16**
Woodchurch. *Kent* —2D **39**
Woodcote. *Oxon* —3C **15**
Woodcott. *Hants* —3A **22**
Woodeaton. *Oxon* —3B **4**
Wood End. *Herts* —2B **8**
Woodend. *W Sus* —2A **44**
Woodend Green. *Essx* —2D **9**
Woodfield. *Oxon* —2B **4**
Woodford. *G Lon* —2B **18**
Woodford Green. *G Lon*
—2C **19**
Woodgate. *W Sus* —2B **44**
Wood Green. *G Lon* —2A **18**
Woodham. *Surr* —2C **25**
Woodham Ferrers. *Essx*
—2B **20**
Woodham Mortimer. *Essx*
—1C **21**
Woodham Walter. *Essx*
—1C **21**
Woodingdean. *Brig* —2A **46**
Woodlands. *Kent* —2D **27**
Woodlands Park. *Wind*
—1A **24**
Woodlands St Mary. *W Ber*
—1A **22**

Woodley. *Wok* —1D **23**
Woodmancote. *W Sus*
(nr. Chichester) —2D **43**
Woodmancote. *W Sus*
(nr. Henfield) —1A **46**
Woodmancott. *Hants* —1B **32**
Woodmansgreen. *W Sus*
—3A **34**
Woodmansterne. *G Lon*
—3A **26**
Woodnesborough. *Kent*
—3D **31**
Wood's Green. *E Sus* —2A **38**
Woodside. *Brac* —1B **24**
Woodside. *Herts* —1A **18**
Woodstock. *Oxon* —3A **4**
Wood Street. *Surr* —3B **24**
Woolage Green. *Kent* —1C **41**
Woolbeding. *W Sus* —3A **34**
Woolhampton. *W Ber* —2B **22**
Woolmer Green. *Herts* —3A **8**
Woolston. *Sotn* —1A **42**
Woolton Hill. *Hants* —2A **22**
Woolverstone. *Suff* —1B **12**
Woolwich. *G Lon* —1C **27**
Wootton. *IOW* —3B **42**
Wootton. *Kent* —1C **41**
Wootton. *Oxon* —1A **14**
(nr. Abingdon)
Wootton. *Oxon* —3A **4**
(nr. Woodstock)
Wootton Bridge. *IOW* —3B **42**
Wootton Common. *IOW*
—3B **42**
Wootton St Lawrence. *Hants*
—3B **22**
Worcester Park. *G Lon*
—2A **26**
Workhouse Green. *Suff*
—1D **11**
Worlds End. *Hants* —1C **43**
World's End. *W Ber* —1A **22**
World's End. *W Sus* —1B **46**
Wormingford. *Essx* —1D **11**
Worminghall. *Buck* —1C **15**
Wormley. *Herts* —1B **18**
Wormley. *Surr* —2B **34**
Wormshill. *Kent* —3C **29**
Worplesdon. *Surr* —3B **24**
Worth. *Kent* —3D **31**
Worth. *W Sus* —2B **36**
Worthing. *W Sus* —2D **45**
Worting. *Hants* —3C **23**
Wotton. *Surr* —1D **35**
Wotton Underwood. *Buck*
—3C **5**
Wouldham. *Kent* —2B **28**
Wrabness. *Essx* —1B **12**
Wraysbury. *Wind* —1C **25**
Wrecclesham. *Surr* —1A **34**
Wright's Green. *Essx* —3D **9**
Writtle. *Essx* —1A **20**
Wrotham. *Kent* —3A **28**
Wrotham Heath. *Kent* —3A **28**
Wroxton. *Oxon* —1A **4**
Wyatt's Green. *Essx* —2D **19**
Wych Cross. *E Sus* —2C **37**
Wyck. *Hants* —2D **33**
Wycombe Marsh. *Buck*
—2A **16**
Wyddial. *Herts* —1B **8**
Wye. *Kent* —1A **40**
Wyfold Grange. *Oxon* —3C **15**
Wyke. *Surr* —3B **24**
Wymering. *Port* —2C **43**
Wytham. *Oxon* —1A **14**

Yalding. *Kent* —3A **28**
Yapton. *W Sus* —2B **44**
Yarmouth. *IOW* —3A **42**
Yarnton. *Oxon* —3A **4**
Yateley. *Hants* —2A **24**
Yattendon. *W Ber* —1B **22**
Yeading. *G Lon* —3D **17**
Yelford. *Oxon* —1A **14**
Yelsted. *Kent* —2C **29**
Yiewsley. *G Lon* —3C **17**
Yorkletts. *Kent* —2A **30**
Young's End. *Essx* —3B **10**

Selected Places of Interest and other features

❑ Opening times for Places of Interest vary greatly; while some open all year, others open only for the summer season, some only open certain days or even part days. We recommend, to avoid disappointment, you check with the nearest Tourist Information Centre (see page 71) before starting your journey.

❑ This is an index to selected features shown on the map pages, it is not a comprehensive guide. Information within a 5 mile radius of the centre of London is not included in the text.

❑ To keep the maps as clear as possible, descriptive words like 'Castle', 'Museum' etc. are omitted, a key to the various map symbols used can be found on page 1 in the reference. Features within very congested areas and town centres are indicated as space allows, wherever possible, at least with the appropriate symbol; in some instances the text may fall into an adjacent map square.

❑ Every possible care has been taken to ensure that the information given is accurate and whilst the publishers would be grateful to learn of any errors, they regret they cannot accept any responsibility for loss thereby caused.

Abbey/Friary/Priory

Battle Abbey —1B 48
Bayham Abbey, Hook Green —2A 38
Beaulieu Abbey —2A 42
Beech Abbey of Our Lady & St John,
Beech —2C 33
Boxgrove Priory —2B 44
Chertsey Abbey —2C 25
Friars, The (Aylesford Priory) —3B 28
Godstow Nunnery, Wytham —1A 14
Lesnes Abbey, Abbey Wood —1C 27
Lewes Priory —2C 47
Minster Abbey —2D 31
Netley Abbey —2A 42
Reading Abbey —1D 23
Royston Priory & St John the
Baptist Church —1B 8
St Augustine's Abbey, Canterbury
—3B 30
St Botolph's Priory, Colchester —2A 12
St Osyth Priory —3B 12
Ware Priory —3B 8
Waverley Abbey —1A 34
Winchelsea Friary —1D 49
Wroxton Abbey —1A 4

Aquarium

Brighton Sea Life Centre —2B 46
Hastings Sea Life Centre —2C 49
Portsmouth Sea Life Centre,
Southsea —3C 43
Southend Sea Life Centre,
Southend-on-Sea —3C 21
Underwater World, "Birdworld",
Holt Pound —1A 34

Arboretum

See also Garden

Bedgebury National Pinetum, Flimwell
—2B 38
Oxford University Arboretum,
Nuneham Courtenay —2B 14
St Roches Arboretum, Singleton
—1A 44

Sir Harold Hillier Arboretum, Ampfield
—3A 32
Whipsnade Tree Cathedral —3C 7
Winkworth Arboretum, Hascombe
—1B 34

Bird Garden

See also Farm Park, Wildlife Park,
Zoo

Beale Park, Lower Basildon —1C 23
Bentley Wildfowl Reserve, Shortgate
—1C 47
Birdworld, Holt Pound —1A 34
Blean Bird Park, Honey Hill —2B 30
Bohunt Manor, Liphook —2A 34
Busbridge Lakes Ornamental
Waterfowl, Tuesley —1B 34
Earnley Butterflies & Gardens,
Almodington —3A 44
Flimwell Bird Park —2B 38
Springvale Flamingo Park, Spring Vale
—3C 43
Wingham Bird Park —3C 31
Woodside Wildfowl Park & Farm,
Aley Green —3C 7

Botanical Garden

Kew Royal Botanic Gardens —1D 25
Oxford University Botanic Gardens
—1B 14
Wyld Court Rainforest,
Hampstead Norreys —1B 22

Butterfly Farm

Eastbourne Butterfly Centre —3A 48
London Butterfly House, Syon,
Brentford —1D 25
Swingfield Butterfly Centre,
Swingfield Minnis —1C 41
Wootton Butterfly World,
Wootton Common —3B 42

Castle

See also Castle and Garden

Abinger Castle, Abinger
Common —1D 35

Aldingbourne Castle —2B 44
Anstey Castle —1C 9
Ardley Castle —2B 4
Arundel Castle —2C 45
Ashley Castle —2A 32
Benington Castle —2A 8
Berkhamsted Castle —1B 16
Bodiam Castle —3B 38
Bramber Castle —1D 45
Broughton Castle —1A 4
Calshot Castle —2A 42
Camber Castle, Winchelsea —1D 49
Canterbury Castle —3B 30
Carisbrooke Castle —3A 42
Chichester Castle —2A 44
Church Norton Castle —3A 44
Colchester Castle —2D 11
Cowdray Castle, Midhurst —3A 34
Deal Castle —3D 31
Deddington Castle —1A 4
Donnington Castle —2A 22
Dover Castle —1D 41
Eynsford Castle —2D 27
Farnham Castle Keep —1A 34
Folkestone Castle —2C 41
Godard's Castle, Thurnham —3C 29
Hadleigh Castle —3C 21
Hastings Castle —2C 49
Hedingham Castle, Castle Hedingham
—1B 10
Hertford Castle —3B 8
Lewes Castle —1C 47
Odiham Castle, North Warnborough
—3D 23
Ongar Castle, Chipping Ongar —1D 19
Oxford Castle —1B 14
Pevensey Castle —2A 48
Pleshey Castle —3A 10
Portchester Castle —2C 43
Rayleigh Castle —2C 21
Reigate Castle —3A 26
Rochester Castle —2B 28
Saffron Walden Castle —1D 9
St Leonards Tower, West Malling
—3A 28
Sandown Castle, Deal —3D 31
Someries Castle, Chiltern Green
—3D 7

Southsea Castle —3C 43
Stansted Mountfitchet Castle —2D 9
Sutton Valence Castle —1C 39
Swerford Castle —1A 4
Totternhoe Castle —2B 6
Upnor Castle, Upper Upnor —1B 28
Weston Turville Castle —3A 6
Whitchurch `Bolebec' Castle —2D 5
Windsor Castle —1B 24
Wycombe `Desborough' Castle,
            High Wycombe —2A 16
Yarmouth Castle —3A 42

Castle and Garden

See also Castle

Guildford Castle —1B 34
Hever Castle —1C 37
Leeds Castle —3C 29
Lympne Castle —2B 40
Scotney Castle, Lamberhurst —2A 38
Tonbridge Castle —1D 37
Walmer Castle —3D 31

Cathedral

Arundel RC Cathedral —2C 45
Brentwood RC Cathedral —2D 19
Canterbury Cathedral —3B 30
Chelmsford Cathedral —1B 20
Chichester Cathedral —2A 44
Guildford Cathedral —3B 24
Oxford Cathedral —1B 14
Portsmouth Cathedral —3C 43
Portsmouth RC Cathedral —2C 43
Rochester Cathedral —2B 28
St Albans Cathedral & Abbey Church
            —1D 17
Winchester Cathedral —3A 32

Cave

Chislehurst Caves —2C 27
Margate Caves —1D 31
Royston Cave —1B 8
St Clement's Caves, Hastings —2C 49
Scott's Grotto, Ware —3B 8
West Wycombe Caves —2A 16

Country Park

Aldenham Country Park, Elstree
            —2D 17
Bayhurst Wood Country Park,
            Harefield —3C 17
Beacon Wood Country Park, Bean
            —1D 27
Bedfont Lakes Country Park,
            East Bedfont —1C 25
Belhus Woods Country Park,
            South Ockendon —3D 19
Black Park Country Park, Iver Heath
            —3C 17
Box Hill Country Park, Dorking —3D 25
Brockhill Country Park, Pedlinge
            —2B 40
Buchan Country Park, Broadfield
            —2A 36
California Country Park,
            Arborfield Garrison —2D 23
Calshot Foreshore Country Park
            —2A 42
Camer Park Country Park, Meopham
            —2A 28
Capstone Farm Country Park,
            Walderslade —2B 28

Cudmore Grove Country Park,
            East Mersea —3A 12
Danbury Country Park —1B 20
Denham Country Park —3C 17
Dinton Pastures Country Park,
            Woodley —1D 23
Ditchling Common Country Park,
            Burgess Hill —1B 46
Dunstable Downs Country Park —3C 7
East Cliff & Warren Country Park,
            Folkestone —2C 41
Farley Mount Country Park,
            Winchester —3A 32
Forest Way Country Park, Forest Row
            —2C 37
Frensham Common Country Park
            —1A 34
Fryent Country Park, Kenton —3D 17
Goodwood Country Park, East Dean
            —1A 44
Great Cornard Country Park —1C 11
Hadleigh Castle Country Park —3C 21
Hainault Forest Country Park,
            Chigwell Row —2C 19
Hastings (Fairlight Cove) Country Park
            —1C 49
Hatfield Forest Country Park,
            Takeley Street —2D 9
Havering Country Park,
            Havering-atte-Bower —2D 19
Haysden Country Park —1D 37
High Woods Country Park, Mile End
            —2A 12
Holland Haven Country Park,
            Holland-on-Sea —3C 13
Horton Country Park, Ewell —2D 25
Itchen Valley Country Park, Swaythling
            —1A 42
Knebworth Country Park,
            Old Knebworth —2A 8
Lakeside Country Park, Eastleigh
            —1A 42
Langley Park Country Park, Iver Heath
            —3C 17
Lee Valley Park, Waltham Cross
            —1B 18
Lepe Country Park —3A 42
Lightwater Country Park —2B 24
Manor Farm Country Park, Hedge End
            —1A 42
Manor Park Country Park,
            West Malling —3A 28
Marsh Farm Country Park,
            South Woodham Ferrers —2C 21
Northaw Great Wood Country Park
            —1A 18
One Tree Hill Country Park, Dry Street
            —3A 20
Pitsea Hall Country Park —3B 20
Queen Elizabeth Country Park, Buriton
            —1D 43
Reculver Country Park —2C 31
Riverside Country Park, Rainham
            —2C 29
Robin Hill Country Park, Downend
            —3B 42
Royal Victoria Country Park,
            Netley Abbey —2A 42
Seven Sisters Country Park, Exceat
            —3D 47
Shorne Wood Country Park, Thong
            —1A 28
Shotover Country Park, Horspath
            —1B 14

Sir George Staunton Country Park,
            Leigh Park —2D 43
Snelsmore Common Country Park,
            Winterbourne —1A 22
South Norwood Country Park —2B 26
Southwater Country Park —3D 35
Stewartby Lake Country Park —1C 7
Stockgrove Country Park,
            Great Brickhill —2B 6
Stoneywish Country Park, Ditchling
            —1B 46
Sundon Hills Country Park,
            Upper Sundon —2C 7
Thorndon Country Park, Brentwood
            —2A 20
Thorney Country Park, West Drayton
            —1C 25
Tilgate Forest Park, Crawley —2A 36
Trent Park Country Park, Cockfosters
            —2A 18
Trilakes Country Park, Little Sandhurst
            —2A 24
Trosley Country Park, Vigo Village
            —2A 28
Weald Country Park, South Weald
            —2D 19
Weald & Downland Country Park,
            Singleton —1A 44
Wellington Country Park, Riseley
            —2D 23
Westley Heights Country Park,
            Langdon Hills —3A 20
Westwood Woodland Park,
            Netley Abbey —2A 42
Yateley Common Country Park
            —3A 24

Farm Park/Working Farm

See also Wildlife Park

Ashdown Llama Farm, Wych Cross
            —2C 37
Badsell Park Farm, Colt's Hill —1A 38
Bocketts Farm Park, Great Bookham
            —3D 25
Bowmans Open Farm,
            London Colney —1D 17
Brogdale Horticultural Trust, Ospringe
            —2A 30
Buckinghamshire Goat Centre,
            Stoke Mandeville —1A 16
Bucklebury Farm Park —1B 22
Burpham Court Farm Park, Burpham,
            Guildford —3C 25
Bury Farm Centre, Epping —1C 19
Chapel Farm Trail, Westhumble
            —3D 25
Clamerkin Farm Park, Locksgreen
            —3A 42
Coombes Farm Tours (Church Farm)
            —2D 45
Dedham Rare Breeds Farm —1A 12
Dunrobin Stud, Greatstone-on-Sea
            —3A 40
Farmworld, Four Oaks —3C 39
Finkley Down Farm Park, Picket Piece
            —1A 32
Gibbons Farm Rare Breeds Centre,
            Beacon's Bottom —2D 15
Godstone Farm —3B 26
Hayes Hill Farm, Holyfield —1B 18
Homestall Farm, Preston —2A 30
Horton Park Farm, Ewell —2A 26
Jakapeni Rare Breeds Farm,
            Hullbridge —2C 21

Lathe Barn, Burmarsh —2B 40
Little Farthingloe Farm, Maxton
—1C 41
Longdown Dairy Farm, Totton —1A 42
Loseley Park Farm, Littleton —1B 34
Marsh Farm, South Woodham Ferrers
—2C 21
Nepicar Farm, Platt —3A 28
Northcommon Farm Centre, Selsey
—3A 44
Oak Farm Rare Breeds Park,
Aylesbury —3A 6
Odds Farm Park, Woodburn —3B 16
Parsonage Farm Rural
Heritage Centre, Elham —1B 40
Seven Sisters Sheep Centre, Eastdean
—3D 47
Sir George Staunton Country Park
Ornamental Farm, Leigh Park —2D 43
South of England Rare Breeds Centre,
The, Woodchurch —2D 39
Standalone Farm Centre, Letchworth
—1A 8
Washbrooks Farm Centre,
Hurstpierpoint —1A 46
Water Hall Farm & Craft Centre,
Whitwell —2D 7

Fortress

Coalhouse Fort, East Tilbury —1A 28
Dover Western Heights —1D 41
Dymchurch Martello Tower No. 24
—3B 40
Eastbourne Redoubt Fortress —3A 48
Felixstowe `Q' Tower —1C 13
Fort Amherst, Chatham —2B 28
Fort Brockhurst, Hardway —2B 42
Fort Luton, Chatham —2B 28
Fort Nelson, Boarhunt —2C 43
Golden Hill Fort, Freshwater —3A 42
Harwich Redoubt —1C 13
Landguard Fort, Felixstowe —1C 13
Martello Tower No. 1, Point Clear
—3A 12
Martello Tower No. 3, Folkestone
—2C 41
Martello Tower No. 73 (The Wish
Tower), Eastbourne —3A 48
Martello Tower No. 74, Seaford
—3C 47
Newhaven Fort —2C 47
New Tavern Fort, Gravesend —1A 28
Portsmouth Round Tower —3C 43
Spitbank Fort, Southsea —3C 43
Tilbury Fort —1A 28

Garden

See also Historic Building & Garden

Apuldram Roses —2A 44
Barton Manor Gardens, Whippingham
—3B 42
BBC Essex Garden, Abridge —2C 19
Benington Lordship Gardens —2A 8
Beth Chatto Gardens,
Elmstead Market —2A 12
Blake Hall Gardens, Bobbingworth
—1D 19
Borde Hill Garden, Haywards Heath
—3B 36
Bridge End Gardens, Saffron Walden
—1D 9
Broadview Gardens, Hadlow —1A 38
Capel Manor Gardens, Crews Hill
—2B 18

Charleston Manor Gardens, Westdean
—2D 47
Cheslyn Gardens, Watford —2D 17
Chilham Castle Gardens —3A 30
Chilworth Manor Garden —1C 35
Claremont Landscape Garden, Esher
—2D 25
Crosswater Farm Garden, Chart-2A 34
Denmans Garden, Fontwell —2B 44
Doddington Place Gardens —3D 29
East Bergholt Lodge Gardens —1A 12
Emmetts, Ide Hill —3C 27
Englefield House Garden —1C 23
Exbury Gardens —2A 42
Feeringbury Manor Garden —2C 11
Gardens of the Rose, Chiswell Green
—1D 17
Goodnestone Park —3C 31
Great Comp Garden, Platt —3A 28
Greatham Mill Garden —2D 33
Groombridge Place &
Enchanted Forest —2D 37
Henry Street Garden Centre,
Arborfield Cross —2D 23
Herb Farm, The, Sonning Common
—1D 23
Herstmonceux Castle Gardens
—1A 48
High Beeches Gardens, Handcross
—2A 36
Highdown Gardens, Angmering
—2C 45
Hollington Herb Garden, Woolton Hill
—2A 22
Hollycombe Gardens, Liphook —3A 34
Holly Gate Cactus Garden, Spear Hill
—1D 45
Houghton Lodge Gardens, Stockbridge
—2A 32
Hyde Hall Gardens, Woodham Ferrers
—2B 20
Hylands Park Gardens, Chelmsford
—1A 20
Iden Croft Herbs, Staplehurst —1B 38
Jenkyn Place Gardens, Bentley
—1D 33
Leigh Park Gardens —2D 43
Leonardslee Gardens, Crabtree
—3A 36
Maldon Millennium Garden —1C 21
Mark Hall Gardens, Harlow —3C 9
Marle Place Gardens & Herb Nursery,
Hazel Street —2A 38
Merriments Gardens, Hurst Green
—3B 38
Moorlands, Friar's Gate —2C 37
Mount Ephraim, Boughton under Blean
—3A 30
Northbourne Court Garden —3D 31
Nymans Garden, Handcross —3A 36
Orpington Priory Gardens —2C 27
Owl House Gardens, Lamberhurst
—2A 38
Painshill Park, Cobham —3C 25
Paradise Centre Gardens, Lamarsh
—1C 11
Pashley Manor, Ticehurst —3B 38
Petersfield Physic Garden —3D 33
Pines Garden, The, St Margaret's at
Cliffe —1D 41
Poplar Lane Thompson & Morgan Trial
Gardens, Chantry —1B 12
Ramster Garden, Ramsnest Common
—2B 34

Riverhill House Gardens, Sevenoaks
—3D 27
Royston Priory Gardens —1B 8
St John's Jerusalem Garden,
Sutton at Hone —2D 27
St Osyth Priory Gardens —3B 12
Saling Hall Garden, Great Saling-1B 10
Savill Garden, Englefield Green
—1B 24
Sheffield Park Garden,
Sheffield Green —3C 37
Sir Harold Hillier Gardens, Ampfield
—3A 32
Sissinghurst Castle Garden —2C 39
Southover Grange Gardens, Lewes
—2C 47
Spains Hall Garden, Finchingfield
—1A 10
Sprivers Garden, Hazel Street —2A 38
Stockwood Gardens, Luton —3C 7
Stowe Landscape Gardens, Dadford
—1C 5
Sunbury Park Walled Garden —2D 25
Valley Gardens, Virginia Water
—2B 24
Wakehurst Place Garden, Ardingly
—2B 36
Wallingford Castle Gardens —3C 15
Ware Priory Gardens —3B 8
Waterperry Gardens —1C 15
West Dean Gardens —1A 44
Wisley Royal Horticultural Society
Gardens —3C 25
Wootton Fountain World,
Wootton Common —3B 42
Yalding Organic Gardens —1A 38

Hill Figure

See also Prehistoric Monument

Bledlow Cross —1D 15
Ditchling Cross, Plumpton —1B 46
Litlington White Horse —2D 47
Long Man of Wilmington, The —2D 47
Watlington White Mark —2D 15
Whipsnade White Lion —3B 6
Whiteleaf Cross, Princes Risborough
—1A 16
Woolbury Flint Horse, Stockbridge
—2A 32
Wye Crown —1A 40

Hill Fort

Beacon Hill Hill Fort, Ivinghoe —3B 6
Beacon Hill Hill Fort, Treyford —1A 44
Chanctonbury Ring Hill Fort,
Washington —1D 45
Cholesbury Camp Hill Fort —1B 16
Cissbury Ring Hill Fort, Findon
—2D 45
Devil's Dyke Hill Fort, Poynings
—1A 46
Highdown Hill Hill Fort, Angmering
—2C 45
Oldbury Hill Fort, Ightham —3D 27
Old Winchester Hill Hill Fort, Warnford
—3C 33
Rainsborough Camp Hill Fort, Aynho
—1B 4
Trundle Hill Fort, The, Singleton
—1A 44
Wolstonbury Hill Hill Fort, Pyecombe
—1A 46

Woolbury Camp Hill Fort, Stockbridge
—2A 32

Historic Building

See also Historic Building & Garden

Abingdon County Hall —2A 14
Albury Park, Shere —1C 35
Ardington House —3A 14
Arreton Manor —3B 42
Audley End House —1D 9
Avington Park, Itchen Abbas —2B 32
Aylesbury King's Head Hotel —3A 6
Aynhoe Park —1B 4
Basildon Park, Lower Basildon —1C 23
Bishop's Waltham Palace —1B 42
Brading Old Town Hall —3C 43
Broadlands, Romsey —3A 32
Canterbury Eastbridge Hospital
—3B 30
Carew Manor & Dovecote, Beddington
—2A 26
Chatley Heath Semaphore Tower,
Martyr's Green —3C 25
Chicksands Priory, Shefford —1D 7
Chiddingstone Castle —1C 37
Chiswick House —1A 26
Claydon House, Middle Claydon —2D 5
Coggeshall Grange Barn —2C 11
Cowdray Ruins, Midhurst —3A 34
Cressing Temple Barn, Cressing
—3B 10
Danny, Hurstpierpoint —1A 46
Dover Maison Dieu —1D 41
Down House, Downe —2C 27
Dutch Cottage, The, Rayleigh —2C 21
Eltham Palace —1C 27
Farnham Castle —1A 34
Fawley Court, Henley-on-Thames
—3D 15
Filching Manor, Wannock —2D 47
Firle Place, West Firle —2C 47
Flatford Bridge Cottage, East Bergholt
—1A 12
Fordwich Town Hall —3B 30
Forty Hall, Enfield —2B 18
Glynde Place —2C 47
Goodwood House, Waterbeach
—2A 44
Gorhambury, St Albans —1D 17
Gosfield Hall —2B 10
Grange, The, Northington —2B 32
Greathed Manor, Dormansland
—1C 37
Great Maytham Hall, Rolvenden Layne
—2C 39
Guildford Guildhall —1B 34
Hadleigh Guildhall —1A 12
Hammerwood Park —2C 37
Hatfield House —1A 18
Hogarth's House, Chiswick —1A 26
Houghton House, Ampthill —1C 7
Hughenden Manor, High Wycombe
—2A 16
Jordans Meeting House —2B 16
Kew Palace —1D 25
Kidbrooke Park & Repton Grounds,
Forest Row —2C 37
King John's House, Romsey —3A 32
Leith Hill Tower, Coldharbour —1D 35
Long Crendon Courthouse —1C 15
Maidstone Archbishop's Palace &
Heritage Centre —3B 28
Mapledurham House —1C 23

Marble Hill House, Twickenham
—1D 25
Mentmore Towers —3B 6
Milton Manor House —2A 14
Milton's Cottage, Chalfont St Giles
—2B 16
Nether Winchenden House,
Lower Winchendon —3D 5
New College of Cobham —2A 28
Newtown Old Town Hall —3A 42
Old Gorhambury House, St Albans
—1D 17
Old House, The, Rochford —2C 21
Old Soar Manor, Plaxtol —3A 28
Osborne House, East Cowes —3B 42
Ospringe Maison Dieu —2A 30
Osterley Park House —1D 25
Paycocke's, Coggeshall —2C 11
Petworth House —3B 34
Princes Risborough Manor House
—1A 16
Priors Hall Barn, Widdington —1D 9
Queen Charlotte's Cottage,
Richmond Upon Thames —1D 25
Queen Elizabeth's Hunting Lodge,
Chingford —2B 18
Queen's House, The, Greenwich
—1B 26
Radcliffe Camera, Oxford —1B 14
Rainham Hall —3D 19
Ranger's House, Blackheath —1B 26
Reculver Towers —2C 31
Rye House Gatehouse, Hoddesdon
—3B 8
Sackville College, East Grinstead
—2B 36
St Albans Clocktower —1D 17
St Edmund Hall, Oxford —1B 14
St Giles Leper Hospital, Maldon
—1C 21
St John's Abbey Gate, Colchester
—2D 11
Shaw's Corner, Ayot St Lawrence-3D 7
Six Poor Travellers House
(Watts Charity), Rochester —2B 28
Southampton Medieval
Merchant's House —1A 42
Southside House, Wimbledon —1A 26
Stowe House, Dadford —1C 5
Strawberry Hill, Twickenham —1D 25
Swiss Cottage, East Cowes —3B 42
Temple Manor, Strood —2B 28
Thaxted Guildhall —1A 10
Titchfield Abbey —2B 42
Uckfield Bridge Cottage —3C 37
Waltham Abbey Gatehouse —1B 18
Whitehall, Cheam —2A 26
Winchester Castle Great Hall —3A 32
Winchester College —3A 32
Windsor Guildhall —1B 24
Woburn Abbey —1B 6
Wolvesey Castle, Winchester —3A 32
Wotton House, Wotton Underwood
—3C 5

Historic Building & Garden

See also Historic Building

Alfriston Clergy House —2D 47
Almonry, The —1B 48
Ascott, Wing —2A 6
Basing House —3C 23
Bateman's, Burwash —3A 38
Belmont, Throwley —3D 29

Bentley House, Shortgate —1C 47
Blenheim Palace, Woodstock —3A 4
Brickwall House, Mill Corner —3C 39
Charleston, Selmeston —2C 47
Chartwell, Westerham —3C 27
Chenies Manor House —2C 17
Clandon Park, West Clandon —3C 25
Cliveden, Cookham —3B 16
Cobham Hall —2A 28
Dorney Court —1B 24
Finchcocks, Goudhurst —2A 38
Frogmore House, Windsor —1B 24
Gilbert White's House, Selborne
—2D 33
Godinton House, Ashford —1D 39
Great Dixter, Northiam —3C 39
Greys Court, Rotherfield Greys
—3D 15
Hall Place, Bexley —1D 27
Ham House —1D 25
Hampton Court Palace, East Molesey
—2D 25
Haseley Manor, Arreton —3B 42
Hatchlands Park, East Clandon
—3C 25
Highclere Castle —3A 22
Hinton Ampner —3B 32
Hospital of St Cross, The, St Cross
—3A 32
Ightham Mote, Ivy Hatch —3D 27
Ingatestone Hall —2A 20
Jane Austen's House, Chawton
—2D 33
Kingston Bagpuize House —2A 14
Knebworth House, Old Knebworth
—2A 8
Knole, Sevenoaks —3D 27
Lamb House, Rye —3D 39
Layer Marney Tower —3D 11
Legh Manor, Ansty —3A 36
Loseley House, Littleton —1B 34
Lullingstone Castle, Eynsford —2D 27
Luton Hoo —3D 7
Michelham Priory, Upper Dicker
—2D 47
Monk's House, Rodmell —2C 47
Moor Park, Eastbury —2C 17
Morton Manor, Brading —3C 43
Nuffield Place —3C 15
Nunwell House, Brading —3B 42
Owletts, Cobham —2A 28
Palace House, Beaulieu —2A 42
Parham House, Cootham —1C 45
Penshurst Place —1D 37
Polesden Lacey, Great Bookham
—3D 25
Port Lympne House, Court-at-Street
—2B 40
Preston Manor —2B 46
Quebec House, Westerham —3C 27
Quex House, Birchington —2D 31
Rotherfield Park, East Tisted —2C 33
Rousham House —2A 4
Royal Pavilion, The —2B 46
St Mary's, Bramber —1D 45
Smallhythe Place (Ellen Terry
Memorial Museum), Small Hythe
—2C 39
Southchurch Hall —3C 21
Squerryes Court, Westerham —3C 27
Standen, Saint Hill —2B 36
Stansted Park, Rowlands Castle
—1D 43
Stanton Harcourt Manor —1A 14

Stoneacre, Otham —3B 28
Stonor Park —3D 15
Stratfield Saye House —2D 23
Swallowfield Park —2D 23
Syon House, Brentford —1D 25
Uppark, South Harting —1D 43
Vyne, The, Sherborne St John —3C 23
Waddesdon Manor —3D 5
West Wycombe Park —2A 16
Wrest Park House, Silsoe —1C 7

Horse Racecourse

Ascot Racecourse —2B 24
Brighton Racecourse —2B 46
Epsom Racecourse —3A 26
Folkestone Racecourse,
 Westenhanger —2B 40
Fontwell Park Racecourse —2B 44
Goodwood Racecourse, East Dean
 —1A 44
Kempton Park Racecourse, Sunbury
 —1D 25
Lingfield Park Racecourse —1B 36
Newbury Racecourse —2A 22
Plumpton Racecourse,
 Plumpton Green —1B 46
Royal Windsor Racecourse —1B 24
Sandown Park Racecourse, Esher
 —2D 25

Industrial Monument

See also Windmill

Bartley Watermill, Bells Yew Green
 —2A 38
Bourne Mill, Colchester —2A 12
Brede Waterworks Steam Pumping
 Engines —1C 49
Calbourne Watermill —3A 42
Chart Gunpowder Mills, Faversham
 —2A 30
Cobham Mill —3D 25
Coultershaw Waterpump,
 Coultershaw Bridge —1B 44
Crabble Corn Mill, Temple Ewell
 —1C 41
Easterford Watermill, Kelvedon
 —3C 11
Ebernoe Brickworks, Balls Cross
 —3B 34
Eling Tide Mill, Totton —1A 42
Ford End Watermill, Ivinghoe —3B 6
Gomshall Mill —1C 35
Haxted Watermill, Edenbridge —1C 37
High Wycombe `Pann' Watermill
 —2A 16
Ifield Watermill —2A 36
Kingsbury Watermill, St Albans —1D 17
Mapledurham Watermill —1C 23
Michelham Priory Watermill,
 Upper Dicker —2D 47
Mill Green Museum & Mill, Hatfield
 —1A 18
Nettlebed Old Kiln —3D 15
Northpark Ironworks, Fernhurst
 —3A 34
Park Mill, Burwash —3A 38
Shalford Mill —1C 35
Swanton Watermill,
 Cheeseman's Green —2A 40
Thorrington Tide Mill —3A 12
Venn Mill, East Hanney —2A 14

Whitchurch Silk Mill —1A 32
Winchester City Mill —3A 32
Woods Mill, Oreham Common —1A 46

Lighthouse

Dungeness Old Lighthouse —3A 40
Harwich Low Lighthouse —1C 13
South Foreland Lighthouse,
 St Margaret's at Cliffe —1D 41

Motor Racing Circuit

Arlington Raceway, Hailsham —2D 47
Brands Hatch Motor Circuit,
 West Kingsdown —2D 27
Goodwood Motor Circuit, Westerton
 —2A 44
Lydden Motor Circuit, Wootton —1C 41
Silverstone Motor Circuit —1C 5

Museum & Art Gallery

Abingdon Museum —2A 14
Airborne Forces Museum, Aldershot
 —3A 24
Aldershot Military Museum —3A 24
Alfriston Heritage Centre &
 Blacksmiths' Museum —2D 47
Allen Gallery, Alton —2D 33
Amberley Museum —1C 45
Amersham Museum —2B 16
Andover Museum —1A 32
Anne of Cleves House Museum,
 Lewes —2C 47
Army Physical Training Corps
 Museum, Aldershot —3A 24
Artillery in the Rotunda, Museum of,
 Woolwich —1C 27
Arundel Museum & Heritage Centre
 —2C 45
Arundel Toy & Military Museum
 —2C 45
Ashford Borough Museum —1A 40
Ashmolean Museum of Art &
 Archaeology, Oxford —1B 14
Banbury Museum —1A 4
Bardfield Cottage Museum,
 Great Bardfield —1A 10
Barleylands Farm Museum, Basildon
 —2A 20
Barlow Collection, The, University of
 Sussex, Falmer —2B 46
Bate Collection of Musical Instruments,
 Oxford —1B 14
Battle Museum of Local History
 —1B 48
Battle of Britain Memorial Museum,
 Hawkinge —2C 41
Bay Museum, The,
 St Margaret's at Cliffe —1D 41
Beecroft Art Gallery, Westcliff-on-Sea
 —3C 21
Benson Veteran Cycle Museum
 —2C 15
Bentley Motor Museum, Shortgate
 —1C 47
Bexhill Museum —2B 48
Bexhill Museum of Costume &
 Social History —2B 48
Bexley Museum —1D 27
Blake Hall War Museum, Bobbingworth
 —1D 19
Blake's Lock Museum, Reading
 —1D 23

Bleak House Dickens Maritime &
 Smuggling Museum, Broadstairs
 —2D 31
Bloxham Village Museum —1A 4
Blue Max Collection, Booker —2A 16
Booth Museum of Natural History,
 Brighton —2B 46
Bourne Hall Museum, Ewell —2A 26
Braintree District Museum —2B 10
Braintree Town Hall Centre —2B 10
Brattle Farm Museum, Staplehurst
 —1B 38
Brentford Musical Museum, Kew
 —1D 25
Brenzett Aeronautical Museum Trust
 —3A 40
Brightlingsea Museum —3A 12
Brighton Museum & Art Gallery —2B 46
British Engineerium, West Blatchington
 —2A 46
Bromley Museum, Orpington —2C 27
Brooklands Museum, Weybridge
 —2C 25
Brook Pumping Station Museum,
 Chatham —2B 28
Buckingham Old Gaol Museum —1C 5
Buckinghamshire County Museum,
 Aylesbury —3A 6
Buckler's Hard Maritime Museum,
 —2A 42
Buckleys Yesterday's World, Battle
 —1B 48
Buffs Regimental Museum, Canterbury
 —3B 30
Burnham-on-Crouch &
 District Museums —2D 21
Calleva Museum, Silchester —2C 23
Canterbury Heritage Museum —3B 30
Canterbury Roman Museum —3B 30
Canterbury West Gate Museum
 —3B 30
Carisbrooke Castle Museum —3A 42
Carshalton Heritage Centre —2A 26
Castle Point Transport Museum
 Society, Leigh Beck —3C 21
Cater Museum, Billericay —2A 20
Chailey Mill Rural Life Museum,
 North Chailey —3B 36
Charlbury Museum —3A 4
Charles Dickens' Birthplace Museum,
 Portsmouth —2C 43
Chatham Historic Dockyard —2B 28
Chaucer Centre, The, Canterbury
 —3B 30
Chelmsford & Essex Museum —1B 20
Chertsey Museum —2C 25
Chichester District Museum —2A 44
Chichester Guildhall Museum —2A 44
Chichester Mechanical Music &
 Doll Collection —2A 44
Chiltern Open Air Museum,
 Chorleywood —2C 17
Cholsey & Wallingford
 Railway Museum —3B 14
Christ Church Picture Gallery, Oxford
 —1B 14
Chuffa Trains Railmania Museum,
 Whitstable —2B 30
Church Farm House Museum, Hendon
 —3A 18
Clock Exchange, South Ascot —2B 24
C. M. Booth Collection of Historic
 Vehicles, Rolvenden —2C 39
Cobham Bus Museum —2C 25

Nature Reserve/Bird Sanctuary

Places of Interest / Various

Dapdune Wharf, Guildford —3B 24
David Evans & Company, Craft Silk
　　　Tour & Shop, Bexley —1D 27
David Salomon's House,
　　　Southborough —1D 37
De Grey Mausoleum, Flitton —1C 7
Devil's Dyke, Poynings —1A 46
Devil's Punch Bowl, Hindhead —2A 34
Ditching Beacon —1B 46
Dover Grand Shaft —1D 41
Dover Knights Templar Church —1D 41
Dover Old Town Gaol —1D 41
Dungeness Nuclear Power Station
　　　Visitor Centre —3A 40
Eagle Heights, Eynsford —2D 27
Eastbourne All Souls Church Brass
　　　Rubbing Centre —3A 48
Ebbsfleet, Richborough Port —2D 31
Essex Showground, Young's End
　　　—3B 10
Farnham Maltings —1A 34
Faversham Stone Chapel —2D 29
Firle Beacon —2C 47
Flitch Way Visitor Centre, Rayne
　　　—2B 10
Folkestone Cliff Lift —2C 41
Foredown Tower Countryside Centre,
　　　Southwick —2A 46
Fort Fun, Eastbourne —2A 48
Gipsy Moth IV, Greenwich —1B 26
Guildford Discovery —1B 34
Harold's Bridge, Waltham Abbey
　　　—1B 18
Harrison's Rocks, Park Corner —2D 37
Hastings Battle Site (1066), Battle
　　　—1B 48
Hastings Embroidery —2C 49
Hastings Lifeboat Station —2C 49
Hatfield Forest, Takeley Street —2D 9
Hellfire Corner &
　Underground Hospital, Dover —1D 41
Hertfordshire Showground, Redbourn
　　　—3C 7
Hickstead Showjumping Course
　　　—1A 46
High Rocks, Rusthall —2D 37
HMS Victory, Portsmouth —2C 43
HMS Warrior, Portsmouth —2C 43
Hog's Back —1B 34
Hog's Back Brewery, Tongham —1A 34
Holly Hill Woodland Park, Park Gate
　　　—2A 42
Hop Farm Country Park, The, Beltring
　　　—1A 38
Hornes Place Chapel,
　　　Appledore Heath —2D 39
Hythe St Leonard's Church Crypt
　　　—2B 40
Intech, Winchester —3A 32
Isle of Wight Brass Rubbing Centre,
　　　Arreton —3B 42
Isle of Wight Model Railways
　　　Exhibition, Cowes —3A 42
Isle of Wight Wax Works, Brading
　　　—3C 43
Ivinghoe Beacon —3B 6
Kennet & Avon Canal Visitor &
　Information Centre, Aldermaston
　　　Wharf —2C 23
Kent County Showground, Detling
　　　—3C 29
Kingley Vale —1A 44
Knights Farm, Swan Street —2C 11
Knole Park, Sevenoaks —3D 27

Lancing College Chapel,
　　　North Lancing —2D 45
Legoland, Windsor —1B 24
Leith Hill, Coldharbour —1D 35
Lewes Living History Model —1C 47
Lexden Earthworks, Colchester
　　　—2D 11
Leysdown Coastal Park,
　　　Leysdown-on-Sea —2A 30
Living World, The, Exceat —3D 47
Lullingstone Park Visitor Centre,
　　　Eynsford —2D 27
Maharajah's Well, Stoke Row —3C 15
Maldon Embroidery —1C 21
Margate Lifeboat House —1D 31
Margate Shell Grotto —1D 31
Mary Rose Ship Hall, Portsmouth
　　　—2C 43
Milton Chantry, Gravesend —1A 28
Mistley Place Park Environmental &
　Animal Rescue Centre, Mistley
　　　—1B 12
Mistley Towers —1B 12
Nazing Glass Works, Broxbourne
　　　—1B 18
New Forest —2A 42
New Forest Nature Quest, Pooksgreen
　　　—2A 42
Norbury Park, Mickleham —3D 25
Nore Hill Pinnacle, Woldingham
　　　—3B 26
North Hinksey Conduit House —1A 14
Old Bodleian Library, Oxford —1B 14
Old Monkton Deserted Medieval
　　　Village, Chilgrove —1A 44
Ongar Greensted Saxon Wooden
　　　Church, Chipping Ongar —1D 19
Oxford Divinity School —1B 14
Oxford Story, The —1B 14
Paradise Family Leisure Park,
　　　Newhaven —2C 47
Petworth Park —3B 34
Philippine Village Craft Centre,
　　　Brookland —3D 39
Pooh Bridge, Hartfield —2C 37
Ramsgate Model Village —2D 31
Raystede Centre For Animal Welfare,
　　　Shortgate —1C 47
Royal Garrison Church, Portsmouth
　　　—3C 43
Royal Military Canal, Appledore
　　　—2D 39
Royal Naval College, Greenwich
　　　—1B 26
Runnymede, Egham —1B 24
Rycote Chapel, Thame —1C 15
Rye Landgate —3D 39
Rye Town Model —3D 39
Saffron Walden Maze —1D 9
St Augustine's Cross,
　　　RichboroughPort —2D 31
St George's Tower, Canterbury
　　　—3B 30
St James' Chapel, Kersey —1D 11
St Mary Magdalene's Tower,
　　　Canterbury —3B 30
Sandham Memorial Chapel,
　　　Burghclere —2A 22
Selborne Hill —2D 33
Shipwreck Heritage Centre, Hastings
　　　—2C 49
Silent Pool, Shere —1C 35
Smugglers Adventure, Hastings
　　　—2C 49
Southend Pier —3C 21

Southend Planetarium —3C 21
South of England Showground,
　　　Ardingly —2B 36
Southsea Model Village —3C 43
SS Shieldhall, Southampton —1A 42
Suffolk Showground, Ipswich —1C 13
Sussex Falconry Centre, Birdham
　　　—2A 44
Thames Barrier Visitor Centre,
　　　Woolwich —1C 27
Toad Rock, Rusthall —2D 37
Tolly Cobbold Brewery, Ipswich
　　　—1B 12
Town & Crown Exhibition, Windsor
　　　—1B 24
Toys Hill —3C 27
Treasure Island, Eastbourne —3A 48
Truggery, The, Herstmonceux —1A 48
Tyland Barn, Sandling —3B 28
Virginia Water —2B 24
Waltham Cross Eleanor Cross-1B 18
Watership Down, Sydmonton —3A 22
Wembley Stadium —3D 17
West Humble Chapel, Westhumble
　　　—3D 25
West Sussex Brass Rubbing Centre,
　　　Arundel —2C 45
White Cliffs Experience, The, Dover
　　　—1D 41
Winchelsea New Gate —1D 49
Winchelsea Pipewell Gate —1D 49
Winchelsea Strand Gate —1D 49
Winchester Heritage Centre —3A 32
Windsor St George's Chapel —1B 24
Woods Mill Countryside Centre,
　　　Oreham Common —1A 46

Prehistoric Monument

See also Hill Figure, Hill Fort

Coldrum Long Barrow, Trottiscliffe
　　　—2A 28
Dane John Mound, Canterbury —3B 30
Five Knolls Barrows, Dunstable Downs
　　　—2C 7
Flowerdown Barrows, Littleton —2A 32
King's Graves Barrows
　(Devil's Humps), West Stoke —1A 44
Kit's Coty House, Eccles —2B 28
Little Kit's Coty House, Eccles —2B 28
Waulud's Bank, Leagrave —2C 7

Railway

Preserved, Steam, Narrow Gauge

Audley End Steam Railway —1D 9
Bluebell Railway, Sheffield Park
　　　—3B 36
Buckinghamshire Railway Centre,
　　　Quainton —3D 5
Chinnor & Princes Risborough Railway
　　　(Icknield Line), Chinnor —1D 15
Cholsey & Wallingford Railway,
　　　Wallingford —3B 14
Colne Valley Railway,
　　　Castle Hedingham —1B 10
Eastbourne Miniature Steam
　　　Railway Park —2A 48
East Kent Light Railway,
　　　Shepherdswell —1C 41
Eastleigh Lakeside Railway —1A 42
Great Cockcrow Railway, Lyne —2C 25
Great Whipsnade Railway, Whipsnade
　　　—3C 7

Hastings East Hill Cliff Railway —2C 49
Hastings West Hill Cliff Railway
—2C 49
Isle of Wight Steam Railway,
Havenstreet —3B 42
Kent & East Sussex Railway,
Tenterden —2C 39
Lavender Line (Isfield Steam Railway)
—1C 47
Leas Cliff Lift, The, Folkestone —2C 41
Leighton Buzzard Railway —2B 6
Mangapps Farm Railway Museum,
Burnham-on-Crouch —2D 21
Mid-Hants Railway (Watercress Line),
New Alresford —2B 32
Mizens Railway, Horsell Common
—2C 25
Romney, Hythe & Dymchurch Railway,
New Romney —3A 40
Ruislip Lido Railway —3C 17
Sittingbourne & Kemsley Light Railway
—2D 29
Spa Valley Railway, Tunbridge Wells
—2D 37
Thames Ditton Min. Railway —2D 25
Volk's Electric Railway, Brighton
—2B 46

Roman Remains

Anderida Roman Fort, Pevensey
—2A 48
Bignor Roman Villa —1B 44
Brading Roman Villa —3B 42
Calleva Roman City Walls, Silchester
—2C 23
Calleva (Silchester) Roman
Amphitheatre —2C 23
Chichester Roman Amphitheatre
—2A 44
Dover Roman Painted House —1D 41
Fishbourne Roman Palace —2A 44
Holtye Roman Road —2C 37
Lullingstone Roman Villa, Eynsford
—2D 27
Newport Roman Villa —3B 42
North Leigh Roman Villa, East End
—3A 4
Pharos, The, Dover —1D 41
Portchester Roman Fortress —2C 43
Regulbium Roman Fort, Reculver
—2C 31
Richborough Castle, Sandwich —2D 31
Richborough Roman Amphitheatre,
Sandwich —3D 31
St Albans Roman Wall —1D 17
Stane Street, Eartham —1B 44
Verulamium Roman Theatre, St Albans
—1D 17
Welwyn Roman Baths —3A 8

Theme Park

Chessington World of Adventures
—2D 25
Dreamland, Margate —1D 31
Legoland Park, Windsor —1B 24
Thorpe Park —2C 25

Tourist Information Centres

OPEN ALL YEAR

NOTE: Telephone Numbers are given
in Italics
Abingdon —2A 14   01235 522711
Aldershot —3A 24   01252 20968

Alton —2D 33   01420 88448
Ampthill —1C 7   01525 842047 /
402051 EXT 2047
Andover —1A 32   01264 324320
Arundel —2C 45   01903 882268
Ashford —1A 40   01233 629165
Aylesbury —3A 6   01296 330559
Banbury —1A 4   01295 259855
Basingstoke —3C 23 01256 817618
Battle —1B 48   01424 773721
Berkhamsted —1B 16   01442 877638
Bexhill-on-Sea —2B 48 01424 212023
Bexley —1C 27   020 8303 9052
Bicester —2B 4   01869 369055
Bishop's Stortford —2C 9
01279 655831
Bognor Regis —3B 44 01243 823140
Borehamwood —2D 17
020 8207 7496
Boship , Lower Dicker —1D 47
01323 442667
Brackley —1B 4   01280 700111
Bracknell —2A 24   01344 868196
Braintree —2B 10   01376 550066
Brentwood —2D 19   01277 200300
Brighton —2B 46   01273 323755
Broadstairs —2D 31   01843 862242
Canterbury —3B 30   01227 766567
Chelmsford —1B 20   01245 283400
Cherwell Valley Services, Junction 10,
01869 345888   M40 —2B 4
Chichester —2A 44   01243 775888
Clacket Lane Sevices, M25
(Eastbound) —3C 27 01959 565063
Clacket Lane Sevices, M25
(Westbound) —3C 27 01959 565615
Clacton-on-Sea —3B12
01255 423400
Colchester —2D 11   01206 282920
Cowes —3A 42   01983 291914
Croydon —2B 26   020 8253 1009
Deal —3D 31   01304 369576
Dover —1D 41   01304 205108
Dunstable —2C 7   01582 471012
Eastbourne —3A 48   01323 411400
Eastleigh —1A 42   01703 641261
Fareham —2B 42   01329 221342
Farnham —1A 34   01252 715109
Faversham —2A 30   01795 534542
Felixstowe —1C 13   01394 276770
Fleet —3A 24   01252 811151
Folkestone —2C 41   01303 258594
Fontwell —2B 44   01243 543269
Gatwick Airport TIC, Horley —1A 36
01293 560108
Gosport —3C 43   01705 522944
Gravesend —1A 28   01474 337600
Greenwich —1B 26   020 8858 6376
Guildford —1B 34   01483 444333
Hadleigh —1A 12   01473 823824
Hailsham —2D 47   01323 844426
Harrow —3D 17
020 8424 1103/1100/1102
Harwich, Parkeston —1C 13
01255 506139
Hastings —2C 49   01424 781111
Havant —2D 43   01705 480024
Heathrow Airport TIC —1C 25
0839 123 456 (Premium Rate)
Hemel Hempstead —1C 17
01442 234222
Henley-on-Thames —3D 15
01491 578034
Herne Bay —2B 30   01227 361911

Hertford —3B 8   01992 584322
High Wycombe —2A 16
01494 421892
Hillingdon, Uxbridge —3C 17
01895 250706
Hitchin-2D 7   01462 434738/450133
Horsham —2D 35   01403 211661
Hounslow —1D 25   020 8572 8279
Hove (Church Road) —2A 46
01273 778087
Hove (Leisure Centre) —2A 46
01273 746100
Lewes —1C 47   01273 483448
Lewisham —1B 26   020 8297 8317
Luton —2C 7   01582 401579
Maidenhead —3A 16   01628 781110
Maidstone —3B 28
01622 602169
Maidstone Services, Junction 8, M20
—3C 29
Maldon —1C 21   01621 856503
Margate —1D 31   01843 220241
Midhurst —3A 34   01730 817322
Milton Keynes —1A 6
01908 232525/231742
Newbury —2A 22   01635 30267
Newport —3B 42   01983 525450
Oxford —1B 14   01865 726871
Peacehaven —2C 47   01273 582668
Petersfield —3D 33   01730 268829
Petworth —3B 34   01798 343523
Portsmouth (Commercial Road)
01705 838382   —2C 43
Portsmouth (The Hard) —2C 43
01705 826722
Ramsgate —2D 31   01843 583333
Reading —1D 23   01734 566226
Redbridge, Ilford —3C 19
020 8478 7145 EXT 222
Richmond Upon Thames —1D 25
020 8940 9125
Rickmansworth —2C 17 01923 776611
Rochester —2B 28   01634 843666
Romsey —3A 32   01794 512987
Rownhams Services —1A 42
01703 730345
Ryde —3B 42   01983 562905
Saffron Walden —1D 9 01799 510444
St Albans —1D 17   01727 864511
Seaford —3C 47   01323 897426
Sevenoaks —3D 27   01732 450305
Southampton —1A 42   01703 221106
Southend-on-Sea —3C 21
01702 215120
South Mimms Services —1A 18
01707 643233
Stevenage —2A 8   01438 369441
Thame —1D 15   01844 212834
Thurrock Service Area —1D 27
01708 863733
Tonbridge —1D 37   01732 770929
Tunbridge Wells —2D 37
01892 515675
Twickenham —1D 25   020 8891 1411
Wallingford —3C 15   01491 826972
Wendover —1A 16   01296 696759
Whitstable —2B 30   01227 275482
Winchester —3A 32
01962 840500/848180
Windsor —1B 24   01753 743900
Witney —1A 14   01993 775802
Worthing (Chapel Road) —2D 45
01903 210022

OPEN SUMMER SEASON ONLY

Buckingham —1C 5 *01280 823020*
Cranbrook —2B 38 *01580 712538*
Foots Cray —1C 27 *020 8300 4700*
Hall Place, Bexley —1D 27
01322 558676
Hastings Seafront —2C 49
01424 781111
Hayling Island, South Hayling —3D 43
01705 467111
Hythe —2B 40 *01303 267799*
Littlehampton —2C 45 *01903 713480*
Marlow —3A 16 *01628 483597*
New Romney —3A 40
01797 364044
Pevensey —2A 48 *01323 761444*
Rye —3D 39 *01797 226696*
Sandwich —3D 31 *01304 613565*
Southsea —3C 43 *01705 832464*
Sudbury —1C 11 *01787 881320*
Tenterden —2C 39 *01580 763572*
Walton-on-the-Naze —2C 13
01255 675542
Woburn —1B 6 *01525 290631*
Woodstock —3A 4 *01993 811038*
Worthing (Marine Parade) —2D 45
01903 210022
Yarmouth —3A 42 *01983 760015*

Vineyard

Adgestone Vineyard —3B 42
Arundel Vineyards, Lyminster —2C 45
Barkham Manor Vineyard,
              Grisling Common —3C 37
Barnsgate Manor Vineyard,
              Heron's Ghyll —3C 37
Barton Manor Vineyard, Whippingham
              —3B 42
Biddenden Vineyards —2C 39
Boyton Vineyards, Boyton End —1B 10
Cane End Vineyard —1C 23
Carr Taylor Vineyards, Westfield
              —1C 49
Chilsdown Vineyard, Singleton —1A 44
Denbies Wine Estate, Dorking —3D 25
Elham Valley Vineyards, Wingmore
              —1B 40
Felsted Vineyard, Bartholomew Green
              —2B 10
Headcorn Flower Centre & Vineyard
              —1C 39

Kent Garden Vineyard, Leeds —3C 29
Lamberhurst Vineyard —2A 38
Leeford Vineyards, Whatlington
              —1B 48
Lurgashall Winery, Dial Green —3B 34
Morton Manor Vineyard, Brading
              —3C 43
New Hall Vineyard, Rudley Green
              —1C 21
Nutbourne Vineyards —1C 45
Penshurst Vineyards —1D 37
Priory Vineyards, Little Dunmow
              —2A 10
Rock Lodge Vineyard, Scayne's Hill
              —3B 36
St Georges Vineyard, Waldron —1D 47
St Nicholas Vineyard, Ash —3C 31
Sedlescombe Organic Vineyard,
              Cripp's Corner —1B 48
Staple Vineyard —3C 31
Tenterden Vineyard, Small Hythe
              —2C 39
Wickham Vineyard, Shedfield —1B 42

Wildlife Park

*See also Farm Park, Bird Garden,
Zoo*

Brambles Wildlife & Rare Breeds,
              Herne Common —2B 30
Mole Hall Wildlife Park, Widdington
              —1D 9
Paradise Wildlife Park, Broxbourne
              —1B 18
Wellplace Bird Farm, Ipsden —3C 15

Windmill

Aythorpe Roding Postmill,
              Roundbush Green —3D 9
Bembridge Towermill —3C 43
Bocking Postmill, Bocking Churchstreet
              —2B 10
Brill Postmill —3C 5
Bursledon Towermill, Lowford —1A 42
Chailey `North Common' Smockmill,
              North Chailey —3B 36
Chillenden Postmill —3C 31
Clayton `Jill' Postmill —1B 46
Cranbrook `Union' Smockmill —2B 38
Cromer Postmill —2B 8
Great Chishill Postmill —1C 9
Herne Smockmill —2B 30

High Salvington Postmill —2D 45
Lacey Green Smockmill —1A 16
Lowfield Heath Postmill, Charlwood
              —1A 36
Margate `Draper's' Smockmill —1D 31
Meopham Smockmill,
              Meopham Green —2A 28
Mountnessing Postmill —2A 20
Nutbourne Towermill —1C 45
Nutley Postmill, Marlpits —3C 37
Outwood Postmill —1B 36
Pitstone Green Postmill —3B 6
Polegate `Ovenden's' Towermill -2D 47
Quainton Towermill —2D 5
Rayleigh Towermill —2C 21
Reigate Heath Postmill —3A 26
Sandwich `White' Smockmill —3D 31
Sarre Smockmill —2C 31
Shipley `Belloc's' Smockmill —3D 35
Singleton Windpump —1A 44
Stansted Mountfitchet Towermil —2D 9
Stelling Minnis `Davison's' Smockmill
              —1B 40
Stock Towermill —2A 20
Thaxted `John Webb's' Towermill
              —1A 10
Upminster Smockmill —3D 19
West Blatchington Smockmill —2A 46
Willesborough Smockmill —1A 40
Wimbledon Common Postmill —1A 26
Wittersham `Stocks' Postmill —3D 39
Woodchurch Smockmill —2D 39

Zoo / Safari Park

*See also Bird Garden, Farm Park,
Wildlife Park*

Basildon Zoo, Vange —3B 20
Chessington Zoo —2D 25
Colchester Zoo, Heckfordbridge
              —2D 11
Drusillas Park, Alfriston —2D 47
Gatwick Zoo, Charlwood —1A 36
Howletts Zoo Park, Littlebourne
              —3B 30
Marwell Zoo, Fisher's Pond —3B 32
Port Lympne Zoo Park,
              Court-at-Street —2B 40
Whipsnade Wild Animal Park —3C 7
Woburn Safari Park —1B 6